D1127488

Introduction

Lincoln Interactive Literature Collections, 4th Grade will introduce your student to a wide sampling of different writing genres. It features examples of short fiction, nonfiction essays, popular media, and much more. In addition to helping your student become familiar with many kinds of literature, these various works will also grow the vocabulary and build crucial comprehension skills that can be applied to any future reading. The book's contents are grouped in such a way that your student can easily compare and contrast similar pieces of writing as well as identify the characteristics that distinguish each genre. This literature collection will help your student to engage with a broad range of themes and genres while providing an enjoyable foundation for learning.

It is important for your student to do the following with each literature piece.

1. Read the title and examine any pictures in the story before reading.
2. Read the short biography about the author, which can be found at the end of the book.
3. Identify and think about the genre of the piece.
4. Read independently.
5. Read aloud to practice fluency.
6. Look up any unfamiliar words.
7. Write down notes and questions that arise while reading.
8. Summarize and discuss the selection after reading, incorporating any notes and questions.

Here are some suggested ways to enrich the reading experience when using *Lincoln Interactive Literature Collections, 4th Grade.*

1. Identify basic story elements such as plot, setting, and character traits.
2. Identify genre characteristics.
3. Compare and contrast different pieces or genres of literature.
4. Do further research into the topic of a nonfiction piece.
5. Have a discussion related to the topic or theme of a literature piece.
6. Identify synonyms and antonyms for vocabulary words.
7. Draw new illustrations to accompany a literature piece.
8. Act out the story like a play.
9. Write an alternate ending to a story.
10. Rewrite a story from another character's point of view.

Contents

~Media~

© National Network of Digital Schools 2012

LINCOLN INTERACTIVE
LITERATURE
COLLECTIONS

4th grade

Daedalus and Icarus

adapted by Sarah Marino
illustrated by Dion Williams

After Theseus of Athens slew the Minotaur in the labyrinth designed by Daedalus, King Minos roared with anger in his palace on the island of Crete. "Daedalus must pay," he shouted. "He is the sole designer of the labyrinth; only with his help could Theseus have found a way through and back out, *and* have destroyed the Minotaur." Minos ordered his servants to punish Daedalus and his son, Icarus, by locking them in the tallest tower in the kingdom.

The tower was a dismal place, especially for a boy of thirteen. Icarus cried frequently, looking longingly through the window and sitting on the rooftop, waiting to be saved. His emotions got the best of him. Sometimes he yelled at his father. He knew it was Daedalus who had given Ariadne the ball of thread that guided Theseus safely through the labyrinth. Fortunately for Icarus, his intelligent, loving father was quite compassionate. He

never scolded Icarus for his complaints and sadness. Instead, he used his wits to entertain them and to devise a plan for escape.

"How will we ever be free, father?" Icarus asked often, his hazel eyes ablaze with an orange glow. "We are in a tower that's impossible to scale, surrounded by water. King Minos would certainly kill us if we were discovered, anyway."

"My son, I will not let us wither away here. I know I can think of something." Daedalus fixed his thoughts on escape. He was first and foremost an inventor, and a skilled craftsman as well. He had invented the labyrinth, which no mortal had successfully conquered and which the Minotaur itself could not even escape. He considered bribing the guards who gave them food, and also trying to attack them, but neither plan seemed sensible. The guards were intensely loyal to King Minos;

they had made a blood pledge to Ares, god of war, that they would always protect Crete and obey their king. Daedalus knew, too, that attempting to attack the guards would surely only cause a commotion that would end with an order for their death.

One radiantly sunny day, as Daedalus and Icarus sat high above the trees on the tower rooftop, Daedalus noticed how many birds were flying around them. He watched them intently as Icarus worked on the bed he had been constructing from hay that the birds had given them after Icarus had prayed to Artemis, goddess of hunting. Icarus had a bit of his father's craftiness in him; he set himself to making odds and ends out of any materials he could gather. Doing so helped him to keep boredom and despair at bay.

"Icarus!" Daedalus shouted. "The birds! Flight is our way to freedom!" The inventor's emerald eyes were alight as he ran to his son.

Icarus grew tense at his father's embrace, always wary of ideas that seemed to come from nowhere. His father had dreamed of many things that never came to be, and Icarus tended to distrust his sudden ideas.

"Father, no man has ever flown like a bird. How could we possibly? Your greying hair betrays your age and your mind, I fear."

"Icarus, you must have more faith in me. We are in this together. I will make it right so that we get out of it together as well." Daedalus knew his son's bitterness and pessimism were growing because of the struggle of being a prisoner. The pain he felt for his son overcame him and he hunched over like a wounded man. But only for a moment would he let himself do so. He straightened and looked back to the birds, knowing that he must be strong for his son.

Icarus saw his father's face fall. He sighed and pushed his bed away, then stood with his father. "How would you do it?" he asked.

"Look at the feathers; I think that is the key," Daedalus said.

Father and son then set about catching many of the birds and plucking some of the animals' feathers. Not wishing to harm the birds, however, they took just three feathers from each and then released them. They spent the next few days gathering them in this way, and eventually had a very large assortment of colored, multi-sized feathers.

"How will you make the wings, father?" Icarus asked. "We are so much heavier than birds."

"I will make them large and strong and bend them so that they move as the birds' wings move," Daedalus answered.

Over the next few weeks, Daedalus carefully built the wings with various tools that he was never without—he was an inventor, after all. He placed the feathers in order by size, with the smallest feathers at the top of each wing. He then sewed them together and used wax to hold them tightly. When the feathers were in order and he was satisfied, Daedalus bent the wings so that they looked just like a bird's, for he knew that this shape must also aid the birds in their flight.

"How do you know they will hold and carry us?" Icarus asked.

"I suppose I don't know for sure, but I have done the best I could. I've been a practicing inventor and craftsman for decades now, so I ought to know something about making things," Daedalus said, trying to amuse his son.

Icarus merely stared at his father. He touched one of the feathers on the set of wings that would be his. While he doubted it would work, he secretly hoped with all of his heart that he would be able to take flight. His eyes grew large, betraying his thoughts.

Daedalus placed a reassuring hand on his son's shoulder. "I think they are ready to be tested. We will go tomorrow morning before first light, when everyone will still be in bed."

* * *

When the first bird sang a note the next morning, Daedalus awoke and roused his son. "It's time."

Icarus moved excitedly throughout their room and followed his father to the rooftop. Daedalus strapped Icarus's wings to him, and then demonstrated how Icarus could help with his father's.

"Listen, Icarus," Daedalus said sternly, seeing his son's excited agitation, "we must concentrate. I will try them first. Do not begin until I tell you. Do you hear me?"

"Yes, father, I understand."

Daedalus closed his eyes and took a long breath. He then opened his wings and began to flap them, just as a bird does. He felt himself lift off of the rooftop and heard his son shout in awe. Several birds flew around him, as if trying to figure out whether he was dangerous or not. They swooped around and around as Daedalus went higher and then soared lower. He went up and down and around the rooftop, and when he was certain that the wings were working correctly, he flew to Icarus and gave him permission to begin.

Icarus spread his wings and faltered at first as he began pumping them. He raised himself from the roof, then felt himself fall and his feet scrape before he at last got the motion correct. He pursed his lips in concentration as he flew higher and higher and then glided down below their tower rooftop. He flew up again, higher and higher, until he heard his father's voice urging him to return. He ignored his father for a few minutes longer before landing on the rooftop.

"Icarus, you must obey me. I told you to return. This is not a game. We are trying to free ourselves, to escape." Though he hadn't meant to, Daedalus could feel the heat of ire flush his face.

"I am good at flying, father. You have made excellent wings. Your skill is unsurpassed. King Minos will be sorry he imprisoned you. He will never know the joy of being a bird!"

Icarus's flattery did not appease Daedalus, who began to untie the wings from his son's arms with more

strength than was needed. "We must practice, Icarus," he said. "Every morning we will practice until we are adept, as if the wings were truly part of us so that we might do it without thinking."

"I will be able to do that easily, father." Icarus stomped to the ladder and lowered himself into the tower chamber.

As they practiced over the next few days, Daedalus explained to Icarus that they needed to stay in a middle path, not too close to the sun or to the sea, but somewhere in between. "The sun will melt the wax holding our feathers, and the sea spray will dampen and weaken the feathers and supports for the thread."

Icarus obeyed his father, but sometimes he flew beyond the middle path and enjoyed the thrill of soaring higher and higher and then gliding as low as the sea. His father would grow angry and reprimand him always after these incidents.

Finally, the morning had arrived when they would leave the tower for good. It was very early and Daedalus secured their wings in the dark as a bird nearby sang a few quiet notes.

"Icarus, I am asking as your father, please obey me. You are my son and I don't want to lose you. Fly with me, son." Daedalus hugged his son tightly.

"I will, father. I can fly with skill—without even concentrating anymore!"

"Do not do that! You must concentrate and follow me. Enough! Do as I say!" Daedalus knelt before his son and looked into his eyes, grabbing his son's wrists. Icarus began to tremble, but he was so excited about the flight that he did not truly listen to his father's command. He did not absorb its significance.

"I will obey, father," he said, staring off into the distance.

Daedalus embraced his son once again before they flew off into the morning sky. Soon they were miles away from the tower and were very close to the end of the island, where they would be safe from Crete's soldiers.

Some farmers and shepherds who caught a glimpse of the human birds were shocked, and one even fainted in his meadow.

Icarus thought he probably looked like a god to those on land. He laughed at their foolishness. His thoughts fed his excitement, his desire to prove himself. He began slowing down a bit so that he was behind his father, then he pumped his wings as hard as he could to fly up far away. *Even some of the gods cannot fly*, he thought. *We are truly like gods*. He wanted to test his skill. He flew in a loop and then down to the sea. His father continued ahead of him. The air whistled in his ears and blew his hair. He had never felt so alive! He could dive and soar and be like a god. He laughed now at his father's caution. *He will never feel alive by being so worried and cautious*, Icarus thought.

He soared higher and higher, through clouds, beyond the hawks, up and up. His father was a speck in the distance. He felt the sun's heat and saw himself as no longer just a boy; his power was beyond human ability. He looked at the sea below him, and then realized he was falling. He pumped his wings furiously but they seemed to be falling apart. The sun had melted the wax, and it dripped from them like blood. Icarus screamed as he plunged into the sea to his death.

Daedalus heard the scream as a murmur far behind him. He turned and, not seeing his son, began to shout his name. He flew back and circled the sea, and was heartbroken to find the feathers floating in a pile, for he understood what had happened. He flew up and down and around the sight, feeling panic ignite in his chest. He knew he had to go on. He wept for his son and pulled himself back onto his course. He found his freedom on the island of Sicily, where he lived until his death and never flew again.

Myth of the Seasons

by Debbie Parrish
illustrated by Dave Rushbrook

Long, long ago, there was no spring, summer, autumn, or winter. At that time, the world was controlled by the many gods and goddesses who lived on Mount Olympus in northern Greece. The chief god, Zeus, had many wives. One of these wives was Demeter. She too was a goddess whose home was on Mount Olympus. In fact, she was one of the original twelve who ruled the world. Gods and goddesses were so special that they were said to be immortal, meaning that they would never die. Human beings were known as mortals because they would die.

Demeter was the goddess of grain, flowers, and all other growing things. The Romans knew her as Ceres. Even though Demeter's home was on Mount Olympus, she mainly lived on the earth so that she could protect and care for all that grows. She was an extremely important goddess to the mortals. Without her, there would be no food. Each day people honored her with music and dancing.

Demeter's job was quite complicated. She had to make sure that Apollo, the sun god, warmed the earth enough to make things grow. She had to remind Zeus, who was also the god of thunder, to send rain for the crops. Demeter kept an eye on the corn to see if it was ripening. She had to nurture the fruit trees to ensure that there would be apples, oranges, and pears. She made the leaves stay green on the trees all year long. She knew that mortals counted on her for shade under the leafy oaks and maples to protect them from the sun's rays. While the other gods and goddesses rested on Mount Olympus, Demeter worked. She had a great responsibility as caretaker of all that grew on the earth.

All year long, the mortals enjoyed the fruits of Demeter's labor. It never grew cold. The gardens always flourished and there was always plenty to eat. Demeter enjoyed her work; however, her chief joy was Persephone, her daughter. Persephone was fair-skinned and smelled of scented flowers. Her fair, white skin was the result of Demeter never allowing the sun to burn her daughter's skin. Persephone's wonderful perfume came from the flowers that Demeter plucked to adorn her daughter's hair. In addition to being responsible for the growing and harvesting of crops, Demeter always made sure her daughter was more beautiful than all other maidens.

Persephone grew up on the island of Sicily. There she would play with the other children of gods and goddesses. One day while Persephone walked along with her friends, she spied a lone, white narcissus. Of all the flowers she had ever seen, this was the most beautiful. Persephone left her friends and hurried to where the lone narcissus grew. She believed that it must be for her. She imagined that her mother had put it there for her pleasure. When Persephone bent down to pluck the narcissus, a gentle wind blew the small flower away from her delicate fingers. Again she reached to pluck this sweet-scented beauty, and again the wind took it from her hand. Not to be outdone, Persephone grasped the blossom and brought it quickly to her nose to breathe in its lovely aroma.

It was then that a terrible thing happened. Persephone felt the earth begin to tremble. She saw the ground split at the spot where the narcissus had grown. The earth opened wider and wider, deeper and deeper. Persephone heard a terrible rumbling coming from the great divide. Steam and smoke poured forth as if it were a volcano. When the smoke cleared, she saw standing before her a tall, helmeted figure. In his right hand, the figure gripped a leash that held a huge three-headed dog, Cerberus, the guard dog of the underworld.

Demeter was not the only god that spent her time far from Mount Olympus. Hades, the god of the underworld, lived not on the earth, but under the earth. Mortals associated this god of the underworld with death, or afterlife. Hades was so lonely that one day he decided he needed a companion. He rose from the depths to claim a wife. The first being Hades saw when the smoke cleared was the beautiful Persephone.

Without courtship and without asking Demeter's permission, Hades took Persephone on his chariot down to the depths of the earth. It all happened so fast that Persephone had no time to protest. One moment her friends saw her plucking the narcissus, and the next moment she was gone. Even if Persephone had protested, it would not have mattered. Death could not be avoided. Hades now had his Queen of the Underworld.

The maidens who had been left behind hurried back to the village and told what they had seen. The news they told was strange, but the girls could not understand why everyone was so frightened. Just then the winds began to blow. A dark cloud hid the sun. Thunder rolled and lightning blazed in the sky. The air grew chilly at first and then cold. Leaves turned orange, red, and yellow on their branches. They then grew withered, turned brown, and fell to the ground. Flowers wilted, and fruit trees dropped apples, peaches, and pears from their boughs to rot in the mud. Crops of wheat, oats, and corn decayed in the fields. For days on end the world grew cold, dark, and dreary. The mortals grew hungry because there was no food to harvest from their gardens. When the young children asked why this was happening, their parents knew the answer. Demeter, the goddess of growing, was not happy.

Demeter was sick with grief. She wandered the earth looking for Persephone. Had she been abducted? Was she dead? What could have happened to her daughter? After searching for nine days with no answer, Demeter flew into the sky to ask Apollo if he had seen Persephone. She knew that Apollo, riding his sun-chariot through the sky, could see everything. Apollo related what he had seen happen in the meadow. Just like any mother might be, Demeter was not only sad—she was angry. Her anger grew more and more, so over to Mount Olympus she flew to find out why the all-powerful Zeus would allow Persephone to be taken from her.

The furious mother demanded that Zeus bring her daughter back to her. The chief god certainly had the power to make this happen, but things on Mount Olympus were very complicated. Zeus was Persephone's father. But Hades, who had taken her, was Zeus's brother. He may have been all-powerful, but keeping all of these family members happy was nearly impossible. He had to find a way to make both Demeter and Hades happy.

It wasn't just his family Zeus had to keep happy. Zeus looked down from Mount Olympus to the mortals who were cold and hungry. He saw their suffering and knew that something had to be done. Demeter, while grieving for her daughter, forgot about the sun and the rain. She cared not that the earth grew cold and that the crops rotted in the fields. When Zeus instructed Demeter to do her job and look after the crops and harvest, she refused. She said that until Persephone was returned to her, she would do nothing.

Zeus then called his brother Hades from the underworld and asked him to allow Persephone's safe return to Demeter. Hades refused. "How can the King of the Underworld live without his queen?" he asked.

Zeus scowled, begged, pleaded, and demanded; but neither Demeter nor Hades would give in. Days turned to weeks, and weeks turned to months. The humans continued to suffer, but the two did not care. Demeter knew that if she held out long enough, Zeus would have to bow to her wishes. After all, Demeter had never taught anyone her secrets of agriculture. Only she could save the mortals from starvation.

When there seemed to be no hope, Zeus thought of a wonderful plan. A compromise! In a compromise, both sides in a disagreement give a little to the other side. Both sides have to give up something that they want. In return, both sides also get something that they want. In that way, both sides win. Zeus called Demeter and Hades to his throne. He looked to Demeter and told her that she had won. She could have her daughter back. He then looked at Hades and said, "You shall keep your Queen of the Underworld." Both Demeter and Hades looked puzzled. How could this be? Zeus warned them that they must agree to his plan if they wanted this to happen. They doubted Zeus's plan could work, but they both agreed that they would follow his demands.

Zeus said to Hades, "You may keep Persephone in the underworld for six months." He looked at Demeter and said, "At the end of that time, your daughter will return to you for six months."

That is how the seasons were formed. During the time Persephone is with Hades, the world is cold, gray, and dreary. Snow and sleet cover the fields, and the seeds lie lifeless beneath the earth just as Persephone does. This is winter.

When it is almost time for her to return, Demeter warms the earth. Crops begin to sprout in the fields, and everything turns green again. This is spring. In summer, Persephone has returned to her mother. The sun is hot; the trees wear their leaves, and the crops bear enough fruit for all to eat. Then comes autumn. Demeter knows that soon Persephone will be leaving her. At this time, Demeter frowns and the air cools. The last fruits of the garden ripen for harvest. Mortals know that they must preserve all the food they can for the long winter days soon to come. At this time, the pumpkins turn orange and trees lose their green to turn bright orange, red, and yellow. Soon the leaves will wither and turn brown. Oaks will drop their acorns, and maples will launch their winged-seeds to the air. The leaves, the acorns, and all of the seeds of the earth will lie buried until it is time for Hades to share Persephone with Demeter come springtime.

Pandora's Box

adapted by Jill Fisher
illustrated by Kevin Dinello

Once long ago, Zeus was extremely angry. Zeus was the god of the sky and king of all of the Olympians. The Olympians consisted of twelve gods who had overthrown the Titans and become the rulers of the world. Zeus was upset because the wisest Titan, Prometheus, had stolen fire from the Greek gods and had given it to man. Prometheus was the creator, protector, and supporter of mankind. Zeus wanted to get revenge and punish Prometheus. So he came up with a plan.

Zeus ordered his son Hephaestus to follow his plan. Hephaestus was the god of fire and forge. Zeus instructed Hephaestus to make him a daughter out of clay. Until then there were no women on earth. Hephaestus made a beautiful woman, and each Olympian gave her a quality. Aphrodite, the goddess of love and beauty, gave her good looks. Athena, the goddess of wisdom, taught her skills and crafts. Hermes, the messenger to the gods, was

ordered by Zeus to teach her to be deceitful, stubborn, and curious. The new, beautiful girl was given the name Pandora, which means the one who bears all gifts.

Zeus instructed Hephaestus to take his new daughter down to earth. Hephaestus took her to Epimetheus, brother of Prometheus. Epimetheus was gentle and lonely. However, he was not very wise. Prometheus, who could tell the future, advised his brother not to accept anything from the god. But when Epimetheus saw the gorgeous woman, Pandora, he was amazed by her beauty. He instantly fell in love with her and they were married.

Zeus gave Pandora a lovely, mysterious box as a wedding present. The box had a large lock on it. He told her that the box contained special gifts from the Olympians, but she was instructed never to open it.

Pandora promised her father she would not open the box. Zeus gave the key to Pandora's box to her new husband, Epimetheus. Zeus was not being kind. He was sure that Epimetheus's curiosity would get the better of him and that either he or his brother would open the box.

Pandora was very interested in what was in the beautiful box. She tried to tame her curiosity, but she could not help herself anymore. She asked Epimetheus for the key, but he said no. Epimetheus was afraid of Pandora's father, Zeus, and did not want to disobey his wishes. He knew Zeus could be very devious.

One day while Epimetheus was sleeping, Pandora stole the key to the box. She immediately opened the mysterious package. Inside, instead of real gifts from the Olympians, Pandora's box contained little winged creatures filled with evil and wickedness. The bad spirits flew into the wind like little bugs. The spirits were made from every kind of disease and sickness, and from hate and envy and all bad things. Before Pandora opened the box, humans had never experienced these awful things. Now crime, poverty, pain, and hunger were spread all over the world. Pandora was very sorry for what she had done. She tried to catch the bad spirits and put them back in the box. Terrified, she slammed the lid closed, but it was too late. They all flew away.

Epimetheus woke up from a deep sleep to the sounds of his crying wife. Pandora confessed to stealing the key while he was asleep and opening the box she had promised her father she would leave closed forever. She told her husband about all of the ugly creatures that had flown out. She described how she had tried to catch them, but there were too many and they got away.

Then she opened the box to show him how empty it was. Only it was not empty. There was one last, tiny creature that flew out. It was not ugly like the evil spirits. In fact, it was beautiful. This wonderful creature was Hope. Hope told Pandora that she was good and her goal was to heal the wounds of the body and soul. Hope managed to fly away and go all over the world. She cured diseases and healed wounds. However, because she escaped much later than the evil creatures, Hope was always the last one to arrive. In a way, though, this was lucky. Because Hope came late, when people were troubled by problems, and when they seemed to lose their health and their possessions, their hope often still remained.

Mythological Terms and Selected Characters

Terms and Places

Cerberus {sur'-bur-uhs}: three-headed guard dog of the underworld
Crete: the largest island in Greece
Mortals: humans
Mount Olympus: the highest mountain in Greece and home to the twelve gods that rule the world
Titans {ty'-tuhns}: early rulers of the earth, overthrown by the twelve Olympians
The twelve Olympians: young gods who overthrew the Titans and made Mount Olympus their home: Ares, Aphrodite, Apollo, Artemis, Athena, Demeter, Dionysus, Hephaestus, Hera, Hermes, Poseidon, and Zeus

Featured Gods

Aphrodite {af-roh-dy'-tee}: goddess of love
Apollo {a-pol'-lo}: god of the sun and music
Athena {a-thee'na}: goddess of wisdom
Demeter {dih-mee'-tur}: goddess of grain and harvest
Hades {hay'-deez}: a non-Olympian god; king of the underworld and god of the dead
Hephaestus {huh-fes'-tuhs}: son of Zeus and god of fire
Hermes {hur'-meez}: god of travel and messengers
Persephone {pur-sef'-uh-nee}: queen of the underworld and the spring
Zeus {zoos}: king of the gods, ruler of Mount Olympus, and controller of lightning, thunder, law, and fate

Titans

Epimetheus {ep-ee-mee'-thee-us}: dim-witted brother of Prometheus
Prometheus {proh-mee'-thee-uhs}: the wisest Titan, who created mankind and gave him fire

Mortals

Daedalus {ded'-ah-lus}: a brilliant architect and inventor who designed the labyrinth, a maze and prison in Crete
Icarus {ik'-ar-uhs}: son of Daedalus
King Minos {my'-nuhs}: ruler of the isle of Crete
Pandora {pan-dohr'-uh}: mortal daughter of Zeus, wife of Epimetheus

The Porcupine and the Firefly

by Nicole Costlow
illustrated by Dion Williams

Penelope was a loner. It wasn't because of her personality; she was as friendly as any porcupine could be. It just seemed to Penelope that no one would give her a chance. Every time she would get brave enough to try to make a friend, whomever it was Penelope said hello to would take one look at her sharp, pointy quills and run in the other direction.

The nighttime crowd in the forest where Penelope lived presented its own challenges. The badgers didn't want to be bothered and weren't very nice. The raccoons were just plain reckless in their search for food. When the fox said he wanted to "have her over for dinner," Penelope was thankful for her quills.

One evening while she was out, Penelope encountered a black-and-white animal just about her size. Feeling braver than usual, she waddled over to the skunk to introduce herself.

"Hello," she said, "my name is Penelope! How are you tonight? What are you having for dinner?" She pointed to the tasty-looking, colorful plant that the skunk was eating.

"Whoa, you scared me! You shouldn't sneak up on me like that!" the nervous animal said, quivering. "You aren't going to hurt me with those sp…sp…spikes, are you?"

"No, I just thought you might like some company," Penelope replied, moving a bit closer.

"Wh-wha-what are you doing? Don't come any closer! I'm warning you…"

"Please don't be afraid," Penelope interrupted. "I promise I won't hurt you. I was just hoping we could be friends. What is your name?" She reached her paw out toward the animal, for a handshake.

11

"I warned you! They don't call me Squirt for nothing!"

Before she even knew what was happening, Squirt the skunk had already turned around, pointed his tail straight up, and filled the air with an awful odor. Sniffing, Penelope felt her stomach turn from the dreadful scent that Squirt had released.

"Cough! Cough! What did you do?" Penelope asked through her coughs.

"I tried to warn you," Squirt replied. "Now leave me alone. I can't trust anyone who looks as prickly as you!"

"I just thought you might like some company," Penelope said. She could feel her eyes starting to well up with tears, but she wasn't sure if it was from the smell or Squirt's reaction to her appearance. "I guess I'll leave you alone then."

"Good riddance!" Squirt shouted, as Penelope walked away sadly.

The next night didn't prove to be much better for Penelope. While nibbling on some tasty tree bark, she noticed a short, plump gray animal heading in her direction, its bright pink nose to the ground as it scavenged for a snack.

"Hi there," Penelope shouted to the opossum.

The animal stopped in its tracks, took one look at her, froze, and fell over. Penelope ran to it as fast as her little legs could carry her to try to help.

"Hey, are you okay? I didn't mean to frighten you! Hello? Heeellllloooo!" But the animal lay very still and did not move a muscle.

"Hello? Mister, are you all right?" Still nothing.

Penelope felt horrible. What had she done? She paced back and forth near the animal for a few minutes, deciding what to do to help him. Finally, she thought it would be best to leave him alone and head toward home. She was terrified that she might make the situation worse. Was she really so frightening that she had made the animal faint? As she began to walk away, she heard a rustling in the brush behind her. When she turned back, she saw the animal's long, skinny tail disappear into the forest.

Penelope headed home that night feeling defeated. No matter what she did or how hard she tried, no one wanted to be her friend. She just couldn't understand it. As she walked, she began to think about all the ways she could try to improve her approach to meeting other forest creatures.

"If these quills just didn't look so scary," she thought. "Maybe if I covered them in mud, no one would notice them. Or maybe if I—"

Smack!

Penelope jumped when she felt something small crash into her forehead. She looked up to find a tiny glowing light in front of her.

"Ouch! Are you okay? I'm really sorry for flying into you. I should watch where I'm going, but I'm just so upset. I hope I didn't hurt you."

"Yes, I'm okay," Penelope said, trying not to laugh at the idea of the tiny insect hurting her. "What's wrong?"

"I'm so tired of it. I just had to get away!"

"Get away from what?"

"My so-called friends," the bug said.

"Why would you want to get away from your friends?" Penelope thought, but was surprised to hear herself speaking the words aloud.

"Well, you see, my parents named me Lightning because they just knew that I was going to have the strongest, brightest flashing light in the forest, just like the lightning when it rains. It turns out that my light is just a faint, dim glow. Now all the other fireflies laugh at it and tease me."

"Well, I don't see anything wrong with your light at all. Look how it shines so brightly on this path," Penelope said as she looked around.

"I guess," Lightning sighed. "Hey, what's your name?"

"What?" she asked, surprised. "You're not going to run away?"

"Well, I've already run into you, so why would I run away?"

"But aren't you afraid of my quills?" she asked nervously.

Lightning flitted around to Penelope's backside and lit up the night to take a peek at her prickly prongs.

"You mean these crazy-looking things? I actually think they go quite nicely with your spiky hairdo."

"My name is Penelope," the porcupine chuckled.

"It's a pleasure to meet you, Penelope, quills and all."

From that night on, Penelope and Lightning became inseparable. They spent their time together in the forest, laughing, playing, and enjoying each other's company. Soon they were the best of friends. Lightning helped Penelope find the most delicious plants to eat on the darkest of nights, while Penelope scared off any creatures looking for a firefly feast. By looking just a little bit deeper, Penelope and Lightning were able to find the true friendship they had both been missing for so long.

It's Party Time!

by Debbie Parrish
illustrated by Brian Cibelli

I have an important decision to make. My nephew, Jeremy, is turning ten next month. Jeremy and his parents moved out of town last summer. They would like to surprise him with a birthday celebration here in town with his old friends. They have asked me to find a place to have the birthday party. I have gone to check out several places, asked some of my neighbors' children, and have even done some online searches to find just the right spot. I visited four or five last week and now I have it narrowed down to two really fun places. One is called Inflation Nation because it has inflatable slides and trampolines. The other place is called Party Times. The names of these two make them sound like they would be great fun! I need to consider the entertainment, the food, the facilities, and the cost of each before I make my final decision.

It was valuable to talk over the phone and look at different websites for information. Both helped me to narrow my choices down, but I still wanted to visit and see each place for myself. After all, I am taking this assignment very seriously. My sister, Jan, trusts me to make Jeremy's birthday a really special occasion. I do not want to let either one of them down. I set aside my whole Saturday afternoon to visit each place before phoning Jan with my decision.

Both places have all of their games and entertainment indoors. That's really good since it is cold and may even be raining the day of the party. They are both nearby, so Jeremy's old friends from school won't have to travel far. Even though one is called Inflation Nation, they actually both have inflatable slides, trampolines, and bouncy balls. Each has an arcade with skeeball, pinball machines, and video games. Party Times and Inflation Nation both have a bowling alley and a miniature golf course.

The managers at both places told me that they could provide all of the food. I liked that we would not have to shop for food and carry it in ourselves. They also said that our party guests could have all of the drink refills they wanted.

I was impressed that each party site checks a guest's invitation before he or she can enter. That seems very safe to me. Also, the games and entertainment stations of each place have adult supervision for safety purposes. Each place also has separate rooms available for eating and opening presents. I am so glad my sister asked me to help with Jeremy's party. He is a great kid, and I want this to be the best birthday ever.

Now, to make a final decision, I needed to consider the cost. I thought both places would be expensive, but they were actually quite reasonable. Each has a set price based on the number of people who are invited. This made it even harder to narrow the decision down. They both appeared to have everything we were looking for.

When I got home, I took out my notes and compared the two places. They looked almost identical until I started jotting down the pros and cons of each. Inflation Nation was much larger than Party Times. The games and inflatables at Party Times seemed to be bunched up on one another. Also, Inflation Nation had huge padded murals on the walls which muted much of the squeals and other party noise. At Party Times, I could hardly hear the manager when he was showing me around. I did, however, like that Party Times would allow us to decorate the separate room to personalize it for Jeremy. We cannot do this at Inflation Nation.

The entertainment at both places seemed to be about equal. Still, Inflation Nation has no limit on the number of times guests can play. Party Times gives tokens; when a guest runs out of tokens, his game time is finished. I also noticed that the trampolines at Party Times did not have safety nets. This worried me. Inflation Nation had safety nets and required each guest to wear a safety harness. Inflation Nation also had a climbing wall that I knew Jeremy and his friends would love.

As I mentioned, the food and beverage choices at both places were about the same, but the price at Inflation Nation did not include cake or ice cream. We could buy them separately or bring our own. The rest of the food in both places looked good and smelled delicious.

The cost to rent each place was nearly the same; both places charged by the number of guests. However, the whole amount for Party Times has to be paid two weeks in advance, and they do not give refunds for guests who end up not being able to attend. Inflation Nation only asks for a deposit and then charges for the actual number of people who come.

Inflation Nation it is! Considering the entertainment, the safety of the facility, the food, and the actual cost of each helped me to make an informed decision. I was so glad that I decided to visit each place before I made my final choice. Even if we do have to bring our own cake and ice cream, Inflation Nation is still the better place. I can hardly wait to tell Jan when she calls tomorrow. I think she will be just as excited as I am. The best part, however, will be seeing Jeremy's face when he walks into Inflation Nation and finds his old friends waiting to surprise him. Nothing will compare with that!

Margaret and Gert

by Sarah Marino
illustrated by Dion Williams

Margaret's Diary

Day 106. Dad keeps telling me it's not going to work, that I might hurt Gert if we continue, but I know she can do it. Yesterday, she didn't stop in the middle; she finished the entire course! Well, she wouldn't do the last jump, but she was just afraid because it had begun to rain. I know she can do it. Her legs are strong enough, and now that she's lost weight, I know it's possible. Sometimes Dad makes me so angry I just run to the barn and cry to Gert. She looks at me like she knows, and she nuzzles her head against my cheek.

Day 117. Today was a great day. We did it. In front of the reporters, Mom and Dad, Leslie, Nigella, Jonathan, and Alan. In front of Mr. And Mrs. Towson and the

girls, and Grandma and Pap. Gert finished the course! And she made both jumps!

She was trembling a little in the beginning, and I was worried that she was going to freeze. She had never run the course with so many people around. I scolded myself for not practicing in front of a crowd, but then I realized it was no time for scolding. I told her to ignore the crowd. I told her it was fine (I was telling myself, too). I told her she could do it and that I loved her no matter what. I could feel her relax as we headed to the first jump. Her legs felt sturdier. She gained a little speed and took the jump with grace, but her legs grazed the crates. She got nervous again, but I kept telling her to settle, and she kept going.

She went through the sand and the grass, slowly but steadily. I could feel the strength in her. It was like she could really hear me and was listening. I knew we would be okay. She kind of raised and lowered her head a few times—her way of telling me she was ready and feeling fine. I just kept saying how great she was doing, coaxing in a tough but gentle way, like Mr. Towson showed me he does with his horses.

Next we went through the cones and she seemed to sway a bit. I was worried that I might slide off of her. She seemed nervous again, and she hesitated after the fourth cone. I kept encouraging, sternly pushing her to keep going. Then she really did stop. It was only for a few seconds, but it felt like hours. My stomach turned over and over. I took a deep breath and kept pushing her. She picked up again and we were through the cones, finally!

Then I started urging her a little more sternly, to get her to go faster for the final jump. She seemed shaky, and I was afraid the cones had made her too dizzy. She listened, though, and we moved several feet.

As we got closer to the final jump, she seemed stronger. It was like a blur. I didn't even realize what had happened until she had done it. We were on the other side and I could hear screams and laughter. I screamed, "Yee-haw," which I've *never* done! I was so happy. I leaned forward and threw my arms around her and squeezed tight. Mom and Dad and Leslie and my friends came and were shouting and laughing, and they helped me down. Dad gave Gert an apple and me some water. Dad said he was proud of me and very impressed.

We had a huge meal after, and now, getting ready for sleep, I feel so tired, but I'm not sure I'll be able to sleep. It was a great day. I hope I never forget it. I hope I can accomplish other things like this in the future, even when people tell me such things aren't possible. I believe in myself.

* * *

Think you know cows? Better think again.
By C. J. Hearst
Associated Press

Well, perhaps pigs might be able to fly after all. Regarding our animal friends, the unthinkable may now be thinkable, given what happened yesterday on the farm of Daniel and Marie Framingham. The couple's daughter, Margaret, 15, successfully directed the family's five-year-old cow through an obstacle course fit for an athletic horse.

Margaret has been designing the course since she was 12 years old. It is quite impressive and unique. Complete with cones in zigzag formation, very tall grass, a stream (albeit quite narrow), sand, and two jumps, it is a course that has proven challenging, while also garnering some attention. A nearby stable owner has used the course several times for a few of his horses, to provide them with exercise and help alleviate boredom.

The teen said she began training Gert, the cow, over two years ago. "I've actually been training her since she was a calf, I suppose, but last summer I wanted to get serious. I knew she was ready."

Mr. Framingham said he knew the cow was different, stronger and more cunning, because it ran away repeatedly as a calf. "She must have knocked down five different kinds of fences—two-rail, three-rail, even a crossbuck fence—but she never went too far. She was feisty but loyal, I suppose. And she took to Margaret from the start."

Still, both parents had their doubts. Although her father was not thrilled with the idea, he also admired his daughter's wit and perseverance.

This reporter was on the scene to watch Gert make her way through the course. She was a bit shaky at first, perhaps because of the gaggle of observers standing around. However, she quickly settled under Margaret's guidance and made her way across the first jump, which consisted of a few old milk crates. Her back legs scraped a bit, but her handler congratulated her and kept her moving successfully.

With much encouragement and prodding, Gert made her way through the grass and sand at a slow but steady pace. The cow almost seemed to nod at times, as if communicating directly with her handler.

There was a bit of a struggle through the zigzag cones as the cow appeared to lose momentum and actually stopped for a moment. Margaret coaxed her through to the final obstacle, the second jump. The teen's face betrayed a slight shadow of fear, but the cow glided easily over the two-rail fence, even though this jump was more difficult than the first.

Cheering friends, family, and onlookers soon surrounded the team. "Yeehaw!" Margaret shouted. Yeehaw, indeed.

Blue Hole

by Michael Scotto
illustrated by Matthew Casper

It was hotter than the F train in August. Not that we were anywhere near the subway, or Brooklyn, or even New York. Actually, we weren't even near August. It was the second weekend in June, and Brand had taken Mom and me to a place called Middlecreek, Pennsylvania. Brand's brother Gil had a farm there, and his whole family was gathered on it for the Cooper family reunion.

You would think a place called Middlecreek would be cool and breezy, but on that Saturday, anyway, you'd have been wrong. There was shade in the picnic tent, but out in the field it was August-hot, and still and sticky as a puddle of maple syrup. As I tossed my horseshoe, I almost expected it to get stuck in the air. I kind of hoped that it would.

It didn't, of course. It just wobbled across the pit like the others and thumped down at the edge of the dirt.

Brand squeezed my shoulder. He was coaching me on how to play. I was playing against Gil's son, Scotty. "Almost, Ed," Brand said. Brand was the only one who called me Ed, but I hoped it would catch on. Mom still called me Eddie, or Edward Franklin when she was upset with me. But I liked Ed. The way I wrote it on tests now was Ed Jordan-Cooper. I guess you could say I was half a Cooper.

"Almost counts, right?" I asked. This was my first game of horseshoes, but I knew that *almost* counted. According to Mr. Davis at school, it also counted in hand grenades, but not in long division.

19

"Well…" he began carefully, squinting like he was worried about hurting my feelings. "It was almost 'almost.'"

Then, of course, Scotty had to chirp in. "Yeah, right, Uncle Brand," he said. Scotty was ten, like me, but you wouldn't guess it from his voice. He whined like a kindergartner. "He hasn't even come close."

I'd only met Scotty once before—last September, when Brand and Mom got married. I didn't like him much then, either. It was his teeth that bothered me. He had this huge gap between his front teeth, and every time the photographer came by our table, Scotty kept using it to do really immature things. Every picture I was in, Scotty was in the background, spitting water from the gap, or sticking the bendy straw from his cola up in it, or pushing his tongue out through it and hissing like a snake. He practically wrecked the whole reception, if you ask me.

And here he was again with that big gap-toothed grin.

"I haven't really been trying yet," I retorted with a scowl. That was a lie, of course. I'd been trying my absolute best to let off a perfect toss. Brand had explained how to throw really well. He was a great explainer. But I just couldn't get it right. It was like my arms wouldn't listen to my brain. I was sure he thought I was a total dummy by now.

"Your turn, Scotty," Brand said.

Scotty turned to him. "Why can't we go to Blue Hole, again?" he whined.

"Blue Hole, what's that?" I asked. At this point, even some dumb hole in the ground had to be better than horseshoes.

Scotty whirled back to me. "Oh, man, it's this great swimming hole near here," he said. "It's in the woods and the water gets really cold. Uncle Brand and my dad went diving there when they were kids. All the Cooper boys go."

"They do?" I asked. This sounded better by the second. I couldn't believe that Brand hadn't told me to bring my swim trunks.

"Hmm," Brand said. He had that careful sound in his voice again. "The water's probably pretty low today."

"It's not," Scotty argued. "Tad and Bart went this morning!"

Brand tilted his head at Scotty. Something in Brand's smirk made Scotty pipe down and take my place at the edge of the pit. I don't know what it was, but I didn't like it. Scotty tossed his horseshoe, and it clanged as it caught the metal post on the other side. I swear, it was like the horseshoe had a magnet in it.

Brand whistled. "Good shot," he said as he gave Scotty a low-five.

"Eleven to zip," Scotty huffed. "Big whoop."

I glanced over at the tent. My mom was helping two other ladies unwrap the potato salad and the macaroni. I didn't know if they were supposed to be my aunts or my step-aunts—I'd forgotten to ask before we got here. What I did know was that it was very weird to be at a Cooper reunion when you weren't a real Cooper. All of a sudden, I was starting to feel just as hot on the inside as I did on the outside. If they had the subway out in Middlecreek, I'd have ridden it all the way back home, no matter how many transfers it took.

"Game's not over yet," I heard Brand tell Scotty. "Ed's pretty sharp. He just might sneak up on you." I turned back to the two of them. Brand pulled a folded up bandanna from his jeans pocket and gave it to me to dry the sweat on my face.

We walked the length of the horseshoe pit as I wiped the wetness from the edges of my hair. I tied the bandanna around my wrist and grabbed a metal U off the ground. I held it up near my face like Brand had shown me. I pulled back, then hefted the shoe toward the spike and hoped for a clang.

Thump. "Wow," Scotty said cheerfully. "You sure are lousy at this!"

"Scott…" Brand warned. But I didn't need Brand to defend me.

I stalked over to Scotty. My mind was racing for a comeback, just the right words to put him in his place. "You know what?" I said. "You really…"

"I really…" he parroted.

"You are really enervating!" I shouted.

Scotty looked at me with confusion. "That's not even a word," he said.

"Oh, yes it is," I replied. I knew it was. I'd lost the P.S. 282 spelling bee over it, because my principal's accent had made it sound like "innovating."

"Go look it up," I told Scotty, feeling six feet tall. "You just might learn something."

Scotty shook his head and stepped over to the pit. "I'm not looking up your silly made-up word," he said, as he bent down to grab a horseshoe. "You are so weird."

And so I shoved him as hard as I could. I don't know why. I'd been called weird before. Once, a kid at school even called me Oddward. But hearing it from Scotty, in that sun, right in front of Brand, too—that hot tingly feeling came back, like my foot had fallen asleep but it was in my stomach, and I just lost it.

We got in one punch each before Brand yanked us apart. He called out, "Nat, honey, hey Natalie!" and I knew I had really messed up, because that was my mom's name.

Mom pulled me by my grass-stained arm, past the picnic tent, past my step-aunts and step-uncle Gil and even step-Grandpa, with his step-oxygen tank. We went into the garage and she sat me down on a lawn chair. She wasn't loud, because the door was open and everyone in the tent could see us, but she didn't need to yell for me to know how upset she was.

"Edward Franklin, what is the matter with you?" she said.

I tried to tell her what happened, but the words kept coming out all wrong. Everything I said just seemed to make her more upset with me.

"We are part of this family now," Mom reminded me, "and you are going to apologize."

If I were a real Cooper, I wanted to argue, *then why didn't Brand tell me about Blue Hole?* But Mom wouldn't have understood. She left me to sit and went back to the tent. Brand touched her arm and talked to her. He said something funny, and Mom laughed. Brand made my mom laugh a lot, which was good because she had a great laugh. It was the kind of laugh that you could watch and just know that it felt great to let out. I got up to find Scotty.

He was sitting at the other end of the tent near the coolers. He had a cold bottle of root beer pressed on the back of his neck to cool off.

"My dad wants me to apologize," he said.

"My mom, too," I said. I knew she was watching right now across the tent.

I pointed to Scotty's root beer. "That looks like a good idea," I said. "Can I have one?"

Scotty made a big show of standing up off the cooler, like he weighed two tons instead of seventy pounds. He opened the cooler and pulled another root beer from the icy slush inside.

"I know a better way we could cool off," I began, as I took the soda. "How about I get Brand to take us to Blue Hole?"

Scotty shook his head at me as if I'd just suggested that we fly to Antarctica. The look made me grit my teeth.

"Why doesn't he want me to go?" I demanded.

Scotty twisted the cap off his root beer and took a sip. "It is kind of scary," he admitted. "I did my first dive a couple weeks ago. My dad wouldn't let me go until I turned ten."

"I'm ten, too!" I said. I didn't like the sound in my voice right then—it reminded me of Scotty's.

Scotty shrugged. "You have to walk on these slippery rocks to get to the hole," he said. "And the hole has sharp rocks all down the sides, so you could get hurt bad if you mess up the jump."

So Brand didn't want me to go because he thought I would screw up. Even though Scotty had done it. Even though every Cooper boy had done it.

"Follow me," I ordered.

Scotty and I marched over to the table where Brand was sitting. My mom was leaning up next to him.

"Friends again, eh?" Brand said.

"Can you take us to Blue Hole?" I asked.

"I have that extra bathing suit," Scotty added. That was a good touch; I hadn't been sure how I'd handle that detail.

Brand glanced over at my mom, and then he got that squint around his eyes again. I was so tired of that careful look.

"It is a Cooper tradition!" I pleaded.

Mom chuckled, but I didn't know what was so funny.

Brand's eyes softened. "Where'd you hear that?" he asked.

"No one told me," I said sharply, so he'd know that he should have.

"It's not far from here, right?" asked Mom.

Even though Brand said nothing, I knew I'd won. Finally, he set his hands on the table and stood. "Grab your trunks!" he declared.

Brand borrowed Uncle Gil's pickup truck and we got on the road. The truck didn't have air conditioning, so we wound through the woods with the windows down. I tried to distract myself from the heat and the itchy waistband of Scotty's swim trunks by watching the view go by. There was more green out here than I knew what to do with. The blinding sun stabbed through the treetops and made spotty patterns on the road. We turned, and the road changed from pavement to gravel as we rumbled deeper into the woods. I watched the trees go by until Brand pulled onto a dirt patch off the road and parked.

Brand pointed to a sign by a path off the road. It said *Blue Hole*. "We walk from here," he told me.

Our sneakers crunched on twigs and pine needles as the three of us walked the path. The air had a sort of earthy scent like I'd never smelled before, not even the times Brand took me on the trails in Central Park. I looked at Brand, who was smiling like he'd just eaten a great meal, and I imagined he was thinking about the air, too.

Soon, we reached a clearing with a rock formation and a big pool of water in the middle. The water flowed in from a stream across one part of the rock. "Feast your eyes," Brand announced.

At first, I didn't understand why it was called Blue Hole. Around the edges, the water was shallow and the rocky surface made it look brown. But then, I saw it. Out in the middle of the pool, the brown suddenly turned a deep crystal blue, like there was dye in the water. "Shoes and shirts off, boys," Brand instructed. He and Scotty began to untie their sneakers. I did the same, then pulled off my t-shirt and untied Brand's bandanna from my wrist.

Brand stepped into the water, followed by Scotty. "We have to cross the stream here to reach the diving spot," he explained. "Be careful, now. It's a little cool, and a little slick."

"I'll be all right," I insisted.

I dipped my bare foot into the stream, and an icy rush shot up my leg. It was like I'd plunged into the soda cooler. I didn't know how the water could have stayed so cold on a day like this.

Scotty must have noticed the shock on my face because he said, "You'll get used to it."

I wasn't so sure, but I stepped onto the smooth rock. Of course, I immediately felt my foot slide away, and I couldn't pull it back to me. I was going to do a split and rip Scotty's swim trunks, I just knew it, but Brand helped steady me before I did. I walked sideways like a crab next to him for the rest of the way.

After a couple more little slips, we reached a spot right near the deep blue water and stopped. "Here we are," Brand told me.

I gaped at him. "We jump off of here?" I said. The rock was more slippery than an ice rink.

Brand nodded. "It's not as hard as it sounds," he said. "What you do is—"

Scotty dove in with a splash. The water hit me, and I felt my heart pound against my ribs. He came up for air and shook the water out of his hair. "Ooo-oooh!" he shouted. "C'mon in, guys!"

I begged Brand for help with my eyes. "Watch me," he said. He described each step as he did it. "You square up your feet, keep them flat for balance, and bend your knees," he said. "The bluer the water, the deeper it is. Keep your arms out ahead, and aim right for the middle of the blue. And then, you dive. Like this."

Brand jumped and went head first into the water. His body completely disappeared for a moment, and then he burst back up.

"Man, oh man!" he said. Scotty splashed him, and Brand splashed back, two Cooper boys having the time of their lives. Brand looked at me and smiled like he had in the woods. "You ready, Eddie?"

Why did he call me Eddie? I tried to ignore it and grip the rock with my toes, but I couldn't do either. *Keep your feet flat*, I reminded myself. Eddie? I took a deep breath and bent my knees. Would my body listen to my brain? There was no *almost* here; *almost* would land me on the jagged edge of the hole, and then Blue Hole would turn to Red Hole with half a Cooper at the bottom. So I only had one try to get it just right. My feet were cold and my stomach was warm, with that tingling feeling that never meant anything good. Brand was waiting, and Scotty was swimming on his back spitting water from the gap between his teeth, like some disgusting fountain. But I had to do it, and do it right. I had to.

I felt a tear hit my cheek. After I felt the one drop leak out, there was no stopping the rest. I burst into tears. They just rushed out of me and down my face, and I couldn't even see; I didn't want to, didn't want to see the way Brand was looking at me. I could just feel myself sobbing and choking on the tears, and I don't know why but they wouldn't stop coming, no matter how hard I tried to tighten up my face. They just wouldn't stop.

A pair of strong hands grasped my shoulders. "It's all right," Brand whispered to me.

He guided me step by step across the slick stone. I wanted to say I was sorry, but I couldn't get a single word out.

"It's okay, Ed, you're okay," Brand promised. I felt my feet step onto a dry rock, and my toes gripped the gritty surface. Brand squeezed me in a hug and held me there for a long time. I didn't even care that he was soaking wet.

"It's all right, Ed, everything's fine."

Finally, I stopped crying and my breathing slowed.

"Scotty!" Brand said. "Time to go."

"Aww, man," I heard him whine. "I'll just go touch the bottom and I'll be out."

After a few seconds I could see again. In Brand's eyes, the careful look was nowhere to be found. They were just strong and warm and right there with me. He picked up his bandanna and handed it to me, and I began to dry my face.

We waited for Scotty to climb out and dry off. Once we were all dressed, we headed back for the truck, Scotty skipping ahead, whistling a tune, Brand and me walking quietly behind.

A Different Goal

by Sarah Marino
illustrated by Dion Williams

The field was a swamp, full of gigantic puddles and gooey mud. It wasn't really fit for play because of the storm the night before, but the girls didn't feel up to asking for a ride to another field. They stood at the side, staring as if perhaps they could will the field to become dry.

"Why don't we practice scoring first? I'll be the goalie and you try to score," April said, walking toward the goal, her long, dark braid swinging behind her.

"I want to practice running and dribbling," Val said.

"We need to practice scoring first," April repeated.

"You're not the boss," Val said. She pulled up her soccer socks and started walking onto the field. "Don't be afraid of the puddles, April. They won't sink you or ruin your pretty shorts."

April rolled her eyes and tried to hide a chuckle. Val was like a nice bossy sister, if there was such a thing. April threw her ball to the ground and began to kick it onto the field.

They dribbled up and down the field together several times, practicing the "inside outside," the "stop and go," and the fake shot. Their shins and calves were covered in mud, but the coolness of the soggy field actually felt nice compared to the muggy air around them on that humid, late-September day.

On the fourth trip down the field, April began to lag a bit. Endurance was not her strongest athletic trait. She was more of a defensive player or goalie, as she was shorter than most other players and a little bit stocky. Sometimes she felt jealous of Val, whose long legs would carry her into the next town over if she had the desire to run there.

The girls were practicing for the new soccer season. They went to different schools, but they both played on the orange team for the Meadville Community League. Their team was made up of kids from ages nine to eleven. Since they were nine-year-olds, they did their fair share of bench warming. They were determined to practice until their skills matched those of the bigger, older kids.

Val stopped on her next trip back down the field, and they decided to practice scoring. April played goalkeeper, and Val missed five shots in a row before getting a goal past her.

Val tossed her head back and let out a frustrated groan, her long yellow hair practically touching her legs. She walked toward April. "Do you think I'll ever be good like Betsy Wright?" she asked.

"I don't know," April said, rolling her eyes. Betsy was a popular girl at her school, St. Rita's, and she was also on the orange team. Ever since the first soccer practice in June, when Val was first introduced to Betsy, Val seemed to bring her up constantly. It had been going on for months now. April looked around the field, waiting for Val to go on about Betsy. She looked toward her house, which was very nearby, and had the urge to go home. Her mother would sometimes shout to them from the back porch, telling them it was time to come in or that it was almost dark. Since April's mother was Chinese, April often felt embarrassed at her shouting; sometimes Val could not understand and would laugh at her mother's accent.

Val lived down the block and on the other side of the street. Val's grandmother had taken care of her ever since her mother moved away to find a job. Her grandmother was kind and funny. She called Val her "muffin" and made cookies for the girls on her days off from working at the store.

Val seemed to be through talking about Betsy, and April suggested that they trade positions so that she could practice scoring. When she was ready, April took a step to kick the ball, and a voice called out, "Hey, you might want more of a running start."

April turned. It was her friend Josh Balaga, who was from Hawaii. He went to St. Rita's, too. He didn't play soccer; his sport was swimming. When he wasn't swimming, he was skateboarding or making model airplanes. He liked to act like he knew all about soccer, though. He was waving as he got off of his skateboard and started running toward them, his wavy brown hair flying behind him.

April sighed. "Josh, we don't need your advice," she said.

"Well, sorry, I thought you might want some help," Josh said.

"Not really," Val yelled. "You can play with us if you want."

Josh looked at April and gave her a big, goofy grin. Some of the kids said that Josh's mom was a hippie, and that she didn't make him take baths or ever get a haircut. They moved from Hawaii about a year ago, when his mother came to take care of Josh's sick grandmother. Josh's dad was still in Hawaii, and he sent gifts and food frequently. Josh was like no one April had ever met. He could be the most annoying person, but also the most fun. He and April spent many afternoons exploring the town by bike and skateboard, Josh giving her the same skateboarding lesson over and over, even though she had terrible balance. Then they would collapse in exhaustion at his house and share a pint of cookies and cream.

"Here," April said, kicking Josh the ball. "You can take it first."

* * *

At their next official game, April got to play goalie for a few minutes in the second half, when the orange team was up 3 – 0 against the green team. It was a beautiful Saturday, and the pine and oak trees around Lewis Field glistened with the morning dew that still covered them. The sun was beaming brightly in the clear, late-morning sky. Val played in the game a lot and had even scored a goal.

Gathering her things afterward, April heard some of the older kids congratulating Val, telling her what a great goal she'd made. Then April heard one of them ask Val to join them for pizza. She looked and saw Betsy Wright smiling at Val. April tried to stop listening. She was only a few feet away from them, but she may as well have been invisible. They took their things, and before she could even say goodbye, Val and the older kids were strolling out into the parking lot.

"Good game, sweetie," April's mother said, coming to help her with her stuff. "Where's Val? Doesn't she need a ride?"

"No," April said, frowning. She picked up her bag and began walking away from her mother.

"Wait a minute," her mother called, jogging to catch up. "What's wrong?"

"Nothing," April said. "Val just got invited to go get pizza with the older kids, and she didn't even say goodbye." April felt her eyes begin to sting and she held her breath, trying to keep the tears from coming.

"Oh, April," her mother said. "I'm sorry. Why don't we go get a treat, too? Dad and Josh would love that." Her mother put her arm around April's shoulder and squeezed her.

April could see Josh and her father waiting by the car. Josh was holding his skateboard and wearing a typical Josh outfit, an oversized t-shirt with shorts. April smiled.

"Hey, good game," Josh said.

"Thanks," April said.

"Good job as goalie, April," her father told her. "We'll practice a little more and you'll be in the game all the time. I'll have another talk with that coach of yours."

"Really, Charles, it's okay," April's mother said, glancing with concern at April and Josh. April knew this look was intended to tell her father to cool it, which her mother probably would have said if Josh hadn't been there.

"Fine, fine," her father said. "Let's get going."

Once they were sitting in the car, Josh pulled out a small plane from his book bag. "Check out my latest model. My dad just sent it. It's a rare one, one of the first flown in World War I."

April smiled at him. She took the plane and admired it while Josh told her about its rapid-fire device and secret door. "It's cool," she said.

Then Josh asked where Val was. April handed the plane back to him and turned to look out the window. "She went for pizza," she said, hearing her own voice getting shaky. *I'm not going to cry*, she told herself.

"Oh, okay," Josh replied, sounding confused.

April knew that if she said anything else, she wouldn't be able to keep herself from crying. She was thankful when her mother turned on the radio. She knew Josh wouldn't be mad if she wasn't very talkative. He took out another plane he was working on.

As they rode to the burger place, April tried to feel excited about the cherry milkshake and cheeseburger she would have, but a knot of distress and sadness had tied itself in her stomach. She sighed, and tried her best to not think of Val.

* * *

April went to school on Monday with that feeling still inside her. She had expected Val to come over on Sunday to apologize, but Val had not. April was already having nervous thoughts about next Saturday's soccer game and what it would be like if she and Val hadn't made up by then.

April could barely pay attention in class. Of course, of all days, the teachers seemed to sense this and called on her to answer questions she didn't know. She couldn't remember whether Alaska was state number forty-nine or fifty; she couldn't recall the difference between transparent and translucent light; she wasn't sure if one hundred was C or M in Roman numerals. She was so happy when art class came and she could make a beautiful picture with watercolors without having to answer questions.

After art class, April sat with Josh and their friend Marta at lunch. Josh's mother usually gave him money to get school lunch, while Marta's mother usually made her peanut butter and jelly, tuna fish, or cheese and lettuce. April had to share food with three other siblings, so her lunches were often meager and dull. One day, her brother had packed her a pickle sandwich and a pretzel rod.

Today she had cheese crackers, a hardboiled egg, an apple, and carrot sticks, none of which she could barter with her friends. She watched with envy as Marta traded Josh her salami and cheese for his Mexican pizza.

Taking a bite of her apple, April noticed Betsy Wright and her friends walking near their table. One of Betsy's friends was a boy named Phil, of whom everyone was a little bit afraid. Phil was in fifth grade and was actually supposed to be in sixth grade, but he had been held back in second grade after a terrible case of chicken pox left him out of school for two months. He was already big for his age, and now, at eleven-and-a-half, he seemed gigantic compared to the fourth graders. He also played on the orange soccer team, though April always stayed out of his way. Some kids said that he and Betsy had been caught kissing behind the gymnasium earlier that school year.

As they walked by, Phil stopped and looked down at Josh's lunch tray. His blondish-brown hair was spiky and stiff, and he had a very round nose that contrasted with his sharp chin and narrow eyes. He belched loudly and looked around at Josh, April, and Marta. Then he looked directly at Josh and said, "Hey, squirt, are you going to eat that cookie?"

"Uh, um, I guess not," Josh muttered, looking at Phil.

April stared at Marta across the table, but Marta was looking fixedly at her pizza crust as if she were studying it for a drawing. Marta was small and mousy, even more so when she was frightened.

"Great, cool," Phil said. As he reached down for the cookie, April made a super-fast arm movement, grabbed the cookie, and stuffed the entire thing into her mouth. Everyone turned and stared at her. She smiled at the look of horror that slowly turned to anger on Phil's face. His cheeks grew red.

"He told me I could have it, chubs," Phil said in a fierce whisper, moving closer to the table and glaring at April. Then he looked at Marta's lunch. Without asking this time, he grabbed a fistful of her corn chips and walked off toward the door with Betsy.

"Wow, April, nice going," Marta said, smiling.

"Sorry I couldn't save your chips." April was feeling a little hurt at being called "chubs," but she tried to ignore it.

"That kid gives me the creeps," Josh said.

"Do you think we should tell Mr. Leonard?" April asked. Mr. Leonard was the teacher on lunchroom duty that day. She looked around but couldn't see him anywhere.

"No, just forget it," Josh said.

"But we learned that we should tell someone about it—about a bully," she said. She couldn't believe Val had left her at the game to hang out with Phil and Betsy.

"What would we say? Um, Phil took some chips because I told him he could have my cookie because he asked for it, but then you ate it?" Josh said. "I don't think that counts as bullying."

"But you saw him. He's rude and gross," April said.

They all let out a round of nervous giggles.

When the laughter wore off, Josh said, "Still, I don't think we have proof that he's a bully."

"He called me a name," April added quietly.

Josh looked at her. "He's a dumb bully."

"I'm afraid to tell on him," Marta said.

April sighed. She was scared, too. It didn't seem like the best choice, but she decided to go along with her friends. They left the cafeteria without telling Mr. Leonard.

* * *

After school, April and Josh made their way down to the soccer field. Josh was going to help April practice her scoring kick and dribbling technique. As they neared the gate to enter the field, April saw a group of kids standing by one of the goals. She recognized Val's yellow hair and bright purple windbreaker. She then realized that Val was with Phil and Betsy and some other kids.

Josh saw it too. "We could try another field if you want," he said.

"Maybe we could play a game with them," April said. She knew monkeys were more likely to fall from the sky, but she wanted to try.

They walked through the gate onto the field. April began to feel tingly all over, as if an electric charge were being sent from her head to her toes. She tried to smile but it felt like too much effort.

Val and the other kids didn't see them until April and Josh were only a few yards away. Val looked at April but didn't say anything, didn't even wave. It was like they were strangers. April wanted to turn and run away, but instead, she decided to do what she had come to do. She didn't care what Betsy or Phil thought. Val was her friend, or so she had thought. April shouted, "Hey, Val! Do you want to play a game?"

The five kids turned to look at her. Betsy said something to Val, and then Val walked a few feet closer to April and Josh. "We were actually going to use the field now," she said.

"Can't we use the field with you?" April asked.

"Hey, why don't you go eat some egg rolls with your little island friend?" Phil shouted. "We're trying to play a game, and we don't need two more girls for the team."

April froze; she felt dizzy and her stomach was queasy. She looked at Josh. His skateboard had fallen at his side. He looked as if he might fall over as well. April nudged him, but his body felt like dough. She saw a glazed look in his eyes.

Then, Val laughed. She didn't just chuckle, either. She threw her head back and let out a shrill sound, like a goose honking. April felt a flash of anger like nothing she'd ever felt before, a wildfire in her blood. She clenched her fists and let out a small scream.

Josh came out of his daze, grabbed his skateboard, and turned to her. "We should go. He's a lot bigger, and he's not kidding."

April only heard the rush of emotion in her ears. She stormed up to Val. "Val, you're going to be like *this*?"

Phil took a few steps and towered over April. "Go home, egg roll."

Val didn't say anything. Her eyes stared back at April, but her lips remained unmoving. April felt a push from the side. She stumbled to the ground.

"Hey, don't," Val shouted.

April stifled tears as she rolled over and tried to get enough balance to stand up. She saw Josh run past her, and then she saw Phil fall to the ground nearby. She stood up but was too late to stop Phil from taking a swing at Josh, which Josh ducked magnificently. As Josh came toward her, Phil came up behind him and pushed him to the ground. April tried to get in Phil's way, but he bent over Josh and threw a punch. Josh rolled out of the way. Then, as he stood up, Phil grabbed Josh's book bag and pulled it off of his back. Josh ran to fight for it, but April grabbed his arm and pulled him with her, toward the gate.

"No, my model!" Josh cried, turning back.

"Josh!"

"Give it to me!" Josh was shouting when April had caught up to him.

"You want your bag, squirt?" Phil said.

"Just let him have it," Val said.

"I don't want to get in trouble," Betsy said.

"Here you go!" Phil said, taking each item out of the bag and hurling it as far as he could down the field.

Josh ran after his things and April followed. He stopped where his bag had landed, and began crawling on the ground.

"Josh, we'll find it," she said, crouching beside him.

"It's from my dad." He pushed a piece of hair out of his face, and April saw his frightened, teary eyes.

April suddenly felt like an ant, small and unimportant in a world where people could throw your belongings—and you—to the ground. She turned and saw that Val, Phil, and the others were leaving the field. She took a deep breath and tried to make the panicky feeling go away. "I'm really sorry," she said. "It was my fault. I shouldn't have made us come to the field."

Josh stopped his search for the plane and looked at her. Then, seeing that the others had gone, he sat down on the grass. "It's not your fault."

She smiled at him, slightly relieved. Then, spotting something in the grass several feet away, she shouted, "Is that it?" She pointed to what looked like a tiny plane in a clump of grass.

"Yes!" he said. He surveyed the damage: a broken wing and a missing window. He could glue the wing, probably, and the window he could replace.

"April! Josh! April!" They turned to see April's mother running toward them.

"Mom!" April shouted. Tears started forming in her eyes.

"What's going on? Is anyone hurt?" her mother said, pulling her into a hug. "I thought I heard shouting, and

I walked past the dining room window and saw Josh push a boy. Then you two were running. I left the house, and Val was walking down the street with those other kids. I asked them what happened and they just kept walking! Was she a part of this?" April's mother finished and gave Josh a hug as well.

April told her mother everything that had happened as best as she could remember—how Phil had instigated and insulted, how no one had stopped him, how he had pushed them and threw Josh's things down the field, and how Val had seemed content to ignore it all and stand there like a statue.

Her mother's eyes grew wide. "What a bully! And I would've expected better from Val. Thank God no one was hurt. I'm going to tell his mother and the school."

"Mom, I don't..." April started.

"I think that might make it worse," Josh said, finishing her thought.

"Well, we're not just letting it go," April's mother said. "Listen, I don't want to discipline you, Josh, or you, April, but next time, remember that it's not worth fighting."

April turned her gaze to the ground as her mother went on, giving them a lesson about not fighting back against bullies, telling them what they had already learned in school. Even though she agreed with her mother, the last thing she wanted to hear now was that they'd done the wrong thing. April felt the tears begin again. She felt sad that they had gotten into a stupid fight, and even sadder that Val had turned out to be not so great of a friend. "I'm sorry," she said. "It was hard. We were so mad. Why did they do that to us?"

Her mother looked at her and sighed. "Sometimes we must forgive people like this. They don't know what they are doing."

"It's not fair," April said. "We didn't do anything to them."

"I know," her mother answered.

"I think I want to tell someone at school," April announced. She looked at Josh. He raised his eyebrows in surprise.

"What if he tries something worse?" he asked.

"Do you think doing nothing would be the best thing to do, Josh?" April's mother asked.

"No," he said quietly.

"It's not always easy to do the best thing. In fact, it's usually difficult. But in the end, you feel better because you did what you felt was right," April's mother said.

"We tried standing up to them today and it didn't really work. Let's try something else," April said.

Josh looked at his plane and then at April. "Okay, I'll help."

April held out her hand and helped Josh to stand up. They started to walk to the gate. It was a grey day, and it looked like it was already seven o'clock at night. The trees branches whispered in a light wind and the neighborhood was quiet.

"I don't know if I ever want to play here again," April said.

Her mother nodded. "It's okay. I would understand."

"You could change to swimming," Josh said.

April looked at him and smiled. "You're a good friend," she said.

"I know," he joked.

They laughed together and walked through the gate, leaving the field behind them.

Fingerprints

by Summer Swauger
illustrated by Dion Williams

Grace sat alone at the lunch table. She looked around the crowded cafeteria and sighed. This was not going as well as she had hoped. She had been at this school for two weeks, and no one had said more than a few words to her. *They'll come around,* she thought. *They're just scared.*

She had been through this before. Grace's dad was in the military, so her family moved around a lot. She had been to two different schools in the past five years. Then, in the middle of her fourth grade year, she had to change schools once more. Now she was here at Franklin Elementary. She thought of her friends at her old school and sighed again. The pep talk that her mother had given her the night before was already wearing off.

"Just be yourself," her mother had said. "Soon everyone will see what a nice, friendly girl you are."

Grace knew that her mother was right, but sometimes she just wished things could be different. She was so lost in thought that she almost didn't notice a group of girls walking toward her table. They were from Mr. Miller's class. She knew the tall girl with black hair leading the group was Jade. She hoped they were coming over to say hello. Quickly, she brushed the cracker crumbs from her hands and silently rehearsed what she would say. *Hi, my name is Grace Harper! What's yours?* She smiled her best smile as the group approached.

But just as Grace opened her mouth to greet them, Jade whispered something to the other girls. They giggled and rushed toward the door. One short, red-haired girl with freckles hesitated in front of the table, but only for a moment. Her green eyes briefly met Grace's before looking away again. She hurried to catch up with the group, not looking back. Grace's heart sank as she watched them go. Even though kids were always this way at first, it never got any easier. She felt hot tears stinging her eyes and blinked hard to keep them back. Thankfully, Mr. Miller blew the whistle for the end of lunch. Grace grabbed her lunchbox and hurried back to the classroom.

* * *

When Grace got home from school, she walked slowly into the kitchen. She tossed her backpack onto the table and slumped into a chair. Her long blond hair fell over her face, but she didn't brush it away. Then she let out the loudest, heaviest sigh she had ever heard.

"What's the matter, honey?" her mother asked, turning from the pot on the stove. "Is everything okay at school?" She knew it hadn't been easy for Grace to switch schools again. Her daughter was well-adjusted for her age, but she still worried about her. All this moving around would be hard for any child.

"Mom, it has been two weeks, and still no one will talk to me," Grace said sadly. The tears that she had held in all day were threatening to spill over. Her mother walked over and pulled Grace close. In the comfort of her mother's arms, she could no longer contain her emotions. Her tears poured out like a flood.

When Grace was born without the last two fingers of her left hand, the doctor had called it a "disability." But Grace was resilient, never letting her missing fingers stop her from trying new things. She had even learned to play the piano and was becoming very good at it. Still, kids at school could be mean, and for Grace, that was the hardest part. She hugged her mother tighter, wishing that she could go back to her old school and be with her friends.

* * *

Later, Grace sat in her room in front of her keyboard. Gazing down, she ran her fingers gently over the smooth black and white keys. She already felt better. The piano was a trusted friend to Grace. It always knew exactly what she was feeling. When she was happy, its notes were soft and sweet as a summer breeze. When she was

angry, the notes thundered from it as she pounded the keys. Today it sounded low and gloomy, just like she felt.

When the family moved, Grace had to leave her piano teacher behind. Mr. Barnes was such a nice man, and he played the piano better than anyone she knew. He had even taught at the Berklee College of Music in his "younger days," as he called them. Grace missed him a lot. They had talked on the phone a few times since she moved away. But it wasn't the same. Sometimes Grace worried that things would never be the same.

* * *

"How many of you will be performing in the spring talent show?" Mr. Miller asked his class the next morning. Several students, including Grace, raised their hands. "Let's have each of you stand up and tell us what you will be performing," he suggested. As they went around the room, the kids had many cool talents. Steven was going to juggle. Caitlin would sing a song. William and Ty were going to do a magic act. Grace was nervous to say what her act would be. *What if they laugh at me?* she worried.

Jade stood up next. "I will be performing an original ballet dance to music from *Swan Lake*," she announced. Some of the girls looked impressed, but the boys didn't get it.

"What is *Swan Lake*?" William asked. Ty waved his arms in the air, pretending to be a ballet dancer, which made several of the other boys laugh. A stern look from Mr. Miller silenced them. Jade ignored their immaturity and explained that *Swan Lake* was a ballet and a piece of classical music written by Tchaikovsky, a famous composer.

As Jade went on about *Swan Lake*, Grace stopped listening. She knew all about *Swan Lake* and Tchaikovsky. In fact, she had been struggling for weeks to master it on the piano. She was getting frustrated with it. Playing the piano had always been easy for Grace. She was not used to having so many problems with a song. But the part of *Swan Lake* she was learning was a difficult piece. The left hand part was fast, and Grace's three fingers had a hard time keeping up. She wished again that Mr. Barnes was around to help her.

Grace was pulled from her thoughts by Mr. Miller's voice. "Grace, would you like to tell us what your act is?" he asked.

"Um, well," Grace started. She stood up and clasped her clammy hands behind her back. She took a deep breath. "I am going to play the piano." She looked around, waiting for the reaction from her classmates.

A few kids snickered. Others just stared at her. The silence felt like it went on forever. Then Jade asked, "How can *you* play the piano?" Grace opened her mouth and closed it again, not sure what to say. She wanted to explain that she practiced every single day. She wanted to tell them that she played better than most kids her age. But before she could find the right words, Mr. Miller interrupted.

"That's enough, class," he said. "Grace. I'm sure you will play very well." Grace sat down in her seat and slumped forward, letting her blond hair cover her face.

* * *

Grace sat alone at the lunch table…again. As she munched on her carrot sticks, she kept going over and over this morning's disaster. She thought everyone already knew about her hand. She didn't think anyone would actually make a comment about it. Grace had wanted to crawl under her desk and disappear. She remembered what her mother always told her. *They aren't trying to be mean; they are just afraid because they don't understand.* She was so wrapped up in her own thoughts that she didn't even notice someone standing right in front of her. When she heard a voice, she jumped.

"Hi," said the voice. It was the short girl with red hair and freckles from yesterday.

"Hi!" Grace replied, surprised that the girl was actually talking to her in the crowded lunchroom. "Do you wanna sit with me?" Grace smiled as the girl pulled out a chair and sat. "I'm Grace Harper. You're Cassidy, right?"

"Yeah, I'm Cassidy Walsh," said the red-haired girl. Then she looked uncomfortably around her.

"You have pretty hair, Cassidy," Grace told her, trying to make her feel more at ease.

"Thanks," Cassidy said, brightening. "But I like yours better." Both girls smiled at each other. "I'm sorry for what happened yesterday," Cassidy said. "I wanted to talk to you, but I didn't want the other girls to laugh at me. But I don't care what they think now. That was really mean of Jade to say something about your hand in class."

"Oh, it's okay. I'm sort of used to it," Grace admitted. She saw Cassidy looking at her hand resting on the table.

"Does it hurt?" Cassidy asked, after a pause.

"No, not at all," Grace replied. "I was just born this way." Grace held up her hands and shrugged her shoulders. "And I never had these fingers, so I don't miss them."

Cassidy looked down at her own hands and then back at Grace's. "Is it hard for you to play the piano?" Grace knew she wasn't asking in a mean way, like Jade had. She thought about it for a moment.

"I don't think it's harder for me than for anyone else," she replied. "It's just different."

"I used to take piano lessons, but I had to quit last year when my dad lost his job," Cassidy said sadly. "I miss it."

"You play the piano, too?" Grace asked in surprise. She couldn't believe that she and Cassidy shared a common interest. She was happy, but sad for Cassidy at the same time. She knew what it was like to have to give up piano lessons.

"Well, you can come over and play my keyboard," Grace offered. Cassidy's green eyes sparkled.

"That would be *so* fun!" Cassidy said excitedly. Grace smiled at her new friend, feeling happier than she had in weeks. The girls continued talking all through lunch, and they promised to sit together every day.

"All right, class," Mr. Miller said at the start of the science lesson. "Today we are going to talk about fingerprints." He paused and looked around. "Look closely at the tips of your fingers. What do you see?" The students all looked down at their fingertips.

"I see swirly lines," Jade said. "They sort of go in a circle."

"Yes," said Mr. Miller. "Notice how your fingertips are not completely smooth. There are tiny ridges on them that form patterns."

"Why?" asked William.

"Scientists aren't exactly sure what the ridges are for," Mr. Miller explained. "But those ridges leave prints on everything we touch. Our fingerprints are very special because each fingerprint is unique. Does anyone know what it means to be unique?"

William raised his hand slowly. "I think it means being different," he said.

"Thank you, William," Mr. Miller said. "You're on the right track." He turned to the chalkboard and wrote the word UNIQUE in big uppercase letters. "Something that is *unique* is the only one of its kind. It is original, unlike anything else in the world." He paused, giving the students time to understand. "Each of our fingerprints is unlike any other fingerprint. Even though we all make fingerprints, each fingerprint pattern is unique."

Grace looked at her own fingertips. *My fingerprints sure are unique*, she thought. *There are only eight of them.*

"Our fingerprints are quite useful," Mr. Miller continued. "Because no two people have the same fingerprints, our fingerprints can be used to identify us. In ancient times, people used their fingerprints to sign documents. They realized that a person could be identified by his fingerprints. Today, we still use fingerprints to identify people. Have any of you ever seen your fingerprints?" The students shook their heads.

Mr. Miller explained that they would do a fingerprinting activity. The students would press each of their fingertips onto an ink pad and then press each finger onto a piece of paper. The ink would leave a visible fingerprint. Then each student would choose a partner and compare fingerprints to see how they were alike and different.

As Grace worked, she looked at her black fingerprints on the page. She thought about how the eight fingerprints identified her. No one would even need to read her name on the page to know which fingerprints belonged to her. *I guess my fingerprints really are special*, she thought.

* * *

That Saturday, Cassidy came over to Grace's house. Grace's mom made them each a bowl of frozen yogurt with fresh blueberries. They sat at the kitchen table, eating and talking.

"So, what are you girls planning to do today?" asked Grace's mother, sitting down with them.

"I'm gonna show Cassidy my keyboard," Grace said. "She used to play."

"Oh, that's wonderful!" said her mother. "Maybe the two of you could play a duet in the talent show."

"Mom, that's a great idea!" Grace was full of excitement. But Cassidy didn't look so happy about the suggestion.

"Well, I used to take lessons," Cassidy explained. "But I had to quit, and I haven't played in a really long time. I wasn't going to be in the talent show." Grace did not want to push her new friend into performing if she didn't want to.

"Thanks for the snack, Mom," Grace said. "Come on, Cassidy. Let's go up to my room."

"Thank you, Mrs. Harper," Cassidy said. The girls wiped their sticky hands, and Cassidy followed Grace upstairs to her room. Cassidy walked up to the keyboard and touched her fingers lightly to the keys.

"Go ahead, play something," Grace told her. Cassidy sat down on the bench, curled her fingers, and slowly played the notes of a scale. Then she played another, and then another. She smiled up at Grace, whose eyes were as wide as saucers.

"That was really good, Cassidy!" Grace exclaimed.

"I guess I remember a little more than I thought," she said happily.

"Let's play something together, just for fun," Grace suggested. She grabbed a sheet of music and plopped down on the bench beside Cassidy. They played slowly at first, letting Cassidy get used to the music. After a few times through the song, Cassidy was playing well.

"Are you sure you don't want to play in the talent show?" asked Grace. "We could play a duet." She gave her friend an encouraging look.

"But you are so much better than me," Cassidy said. "You probably want to play a really hard song."

"Actually," Grace admitted, "I've been working on *Swan Lake*, but I can't seem to get the fingering of my left hand on certain parts. I think that song was written for people with ten fingers." She held up her hands and wiggled her digits.

"No way," Cassidy told her, looking through Grace's music books. "You'll get it. Isn't your piano teacher helping you?" Grace explained that when her family moved, she couldn't take lessons from Mr. Barnes anymore. She hadn't found a new teacher yet.

"You should talk to Mr. Miller," Cassidy said. "I used to take my lessons from him."

"I didn't know Mr. Miller taught piano!" Grace was surprised. "I will ask my mom to call him tomorrow." The girls continued to play for the rest of the afternoon. They took turns playing songs, and even tried out a few duets. Eventually, Cassidy agreed to play a duet with Grace for the talent show. They would play "The Blue Danube" by Strauss. As it turned out, Cassidy enjoyed playing the piano as much as Grace did.

That evening, after Cassidy's father came to pick her up, Grace sat at her piano. Her fingers danced lightly over the keys. The music came out as cheerful as a songbird's happy tune.

* * *

The next Thursday after school, Grace had her third piano lesson with Mr. Miller. She kept glancing at the clock on the wall, waiting for four o'clock. They were working on *Swan Lake*, and Grace had just messed up for what felt like the thousandth time. If she had to play it again, she thought she might scream.

"Mr. Miller, can we work on something else?" Grace asked, clearly frustrated.

"Don't you want to get this one right?" he asked her.

"I can't do it," Grace said. "The left hand part is just too hard and too fast for me." She shut the music book with a thud. She looked up at the clock again. She still had twenty minutes to go.

"Grace," said Mr. Miller patiently, "you don't seem like someone who would just give up." She looked up at him, her eyes glistening with tears of defeat.

"But I've never had to work this hard before," she insisted.

"Well, you've never played something this difficult before, either," he pointed out. "Playing the piano takes lots of practice."

"You sound like my old piano teacher," she said. Grace let herself smile as she remembered their lessons. "Mr. Barnes always said that there are three secrets to playing well: practice, practice, and practice." They both laughed.

"He sounds like a smart man," Mr. Miller said. Grace nodded. She knew that both of her teachers were right. She shouldn't give up. She opened the music book again and turned to *Swan Lake*.

Mr. Miller gave Grace some exercises that would strengthen the muscles of her left hand. If she did them every day, they might help her fingers keep up with the music. They went through the song a few more times, and pretty soon the lesson was over. As Grace closed the door of the music room, she left her frustration behind. She would master *Swan Lake* with her eight fingers no matter how long it took.

* * *

The night of the talent show had finally arrived. All of the performers were crammed into the music room, and everyone wanted to practice their acts. Jade was whirling and twirling around, bumping into Steven and making him drop his juggling balls. The frog from William and Ty's magic act had escaped. They were running around trying to grab it, while girls screamed and climbed onto chairs. All of the commotion was making it difficult for Grace and Cassidy to practice at the piano.

Mr. Miller came in to quiet them. "Ten minutes, everyone!" he yelled. "Grace and Cassidy, you're up first."

Cassidy turned to Grace, her eyes clouded with doubt. "Grace, what if I mess up and everyone laughs?"

"Cassidy, you will do fine," Grace said, trying to comfort her friend. She took Cassidy's shaking hands in hers and squeezed them. "We just played the song perfectly three times in a row. You are *not* going to mess up." Together, they took a few deep breaths.

Just then, Jade dashed into the room. "Mr. Miller! Mr. Miller!" She was in tears.

"What's wrong, Jade?" Mr. Miller asked, worried.

"My piano player just called and said she is stuck in traffic!" Jade shrieked. "She can't get here in time! The show is ruined!" She gasped for breath.

"Don't worry," he said calmly. Everyone was silent. Mr. Miller turned toward Grace. "You've been doing really well with *Swan Lake*, Grace. Do you think you could play for Jade?" he asked her. All eyes were locked on Grace. Jade held her breath.

Grace looked at Mr. Miller uncertainly. She wasn't sure if she was ready to play that song in front of an audience. Her mind was a whirlwind of thoughts. She knew there were many reasons why she didn't want to play that song. It was such a hard song, and if she messed up, Jade would never forgive her. But in that moment, she couldn't think of any reason that she *couldn't* play it. Mr. Miller gave her a reassuring look.

"Grace, I know you can do it," he told her. She knew he was right. With Mr. Miller's help, she had almost mastered it. The exercises she had been doing every night had helped a lot, too. The fingers of her left hand had gotten faster, allowing her to play better.

"Okay," Grace said. She smiled kindly at Jade. "Do you have the sheet music?" While Jade ran to get it, everyone breathed in relief. The show would go on. Only Cassidy looked confused.

"Grace, why would you do that for her after she's been so mean to you?" Cassidy asked. Grace just shrugged. She didn't really know why, but she wanted to help Jade. It seemed like the right thing to do.

Jade returned with the sheet music. As she handed it to Grace, she looked down at her coldly. "Don't screw it up," Jade warned. Then she turned and quickly walked away. Grace glanced wide-eyed at Cassidy, who rolled her eyes. Jade's threat had not helped Grace's nerves. As Grace looked over the sheet music, she tried to ignore her fluttering stomach. *Okay, Grace, you can do this*, she thought.

But she didn't even have time to think about it because Cassidy was pulling her toward the stage for their duet. It was time to start the show. Standing on the dark stage behind the curtain, the girls tried to peek out into the audience. Grace spotted her parents. Cassidy wiped her sweaty palms on her jeans.

"Ready?" Grace asked.

"Ready," Cassidy said. The girls smiled. They hugged each other tightly for good luck and took their seats at the piano. As the curtain rose and the stage lights came on, they heard Mr. Miller announcing them.

"Please welcome our first act to the stage: Grace Harper and Cassidy Walsh, performing a piano duet!" The audience clapped and then grew silent. Grace lifted her fingers and lightly played the opening notes. Cassidy joined in, and they were swept away on the melody of "The Blue Danube." When the song ended, both girls glowed with pride. It had been perfect. The audience clapped and cheered as they took their bows.

After congratulating each other, Grace headed back to the music room to practice *Swan Lake*. Jade's dance was the last act before intermission, so she had some time to prepare. She sat staring at the pages in front of her. Then she looked down at her hands. She tried to imagine the fingers she never had, but she couldn't. All she saw were her hands. These hands had always been good enough for her. *They'll be good enough tonight, too,* she told herself.

Grace practiced the song over and over. Then she headed backstage to get ready for Jade's act. As she stood nervously waiting to go on, she thought of Mr. Barnes and Mr. Miller. Both had taught her so much, not only about playing the piano, but also about accepting herself as she was. She knew they were proud of her. Then she heard Mr. Miller's voice.

"Ladies and gentlemen, please welcome Jade Lee, accompanied by Grace Harper on piano!" As the audience clapped, Grace took her seat at the piano and Jade took her place at center stage. Their eyes met for a split second before Jade turned away toward her audience. Grace took a deep breath and began. As she played, the music came from deep inside of her. It flowed out of her fingertips and filled the air.

When Grace finished, the audience erupted into thunderous applause. Jade had danced very well, and Grace had played perfectly. The girls took their bows and left the stage. As Grace went toward the music room, Jade grabbed her arm. Grace spun around and their eyes met. Jade's face softened.

"That was really good," she told Grace. "I don't think my piano player ever played it that well." She paused, looking down at her toes. Then she looked up again and said, "Thanks." Grace smiled at her, and Jade smiled back. The two girls made their way out into the lobby. Immediately, Grace was surrounded by her parents, Cassidy, and all of the kids from Mr. Miller's class.

"Grace, honey, we are so proud of you!" Grace's mother told her with tears in her eyes. After many hugs, her parents stepped back so that Grace could talk to her classmates.

"Good job, Grace!" William said. Ty gave her a high five. Everyone was talking at once. Even Jade joined in, saying that she couldn't have done her act without Grace at the piano.

Grace had been smiling ever since she had played the last note. She was smiling so big that her face hurt. But she didn't care. Nothing could take away her smile tonight. She looked around at her new friends. They no longer looked at her like she was different. She was just Grace, just unique, just herself.

Waynesboro to Washington

by Sarah Marino
illustrated by Dion Williams

Courtney parked her bike in the backyard and shouted hello to her grandpap, who was already working in the garden. Her friends Jane and Eric were by the porch, nibbling on lemon bars and grapes her gran had given them.

"Courtney, you're late. You're lucky we didn't eat them all," Jane said, smiling, talking, and chewing all at once.

"Very funny," Courtney said, helping herself to a bar from the plate on the picnic table.

"Is your grandpap really going to give us each ten dollars to help in the garden today? I mean, my mom said I shouldn't even take it since your gran has been feeding us all summer, but I hate to work all afternoon in this heat if we're only going to get food. I'm not saying I won't help, I just..." Eric lifted his Orioles cap and then put it back on his head. This was a nervous habit of his. His dark, wavy hair was wet with sweat at his temples.

"Geez, Eric, we aren't going to sweat to death," Courtney said, laughing. "Come on. Let's get started before it's even hotter."

Courtney, Jane, and Eric had been friends practically since they could talk. They had all grown up on the same street in outer Waynesboro, Pennsylvania, about eighty miles north of Washington, DC. Courtney and her mother technically lived in Waynesboro Village, but her grandparents lived here, and for that reason, she basically did, too. In the summer, the three friends were inseparable.

Her grandpap stood near the cabbage, humming an old country song that none of them knew. He gave them each a task and then left them alone.

They worked intently, stopping to joke only now and then, all of them wanting to be finished as soon as possible, to take the money and flee to the pool for swimming and ice cream sandwiches.

* * *

That night, Courtney's mother stood in the kitchen, chopping carrots to put on their dinner salads. She still had her nurse's uniform on; it was the maroon-colored set. Courtney sat at the kitchen table, trying to think of something funny that had happened that day to tell her mom. Before she could think of anything, her mom began to speak.

"Courtney, there's something we need to talk about, honey." She came and sat at the table.

Courtney watched her mother and noticed she was smiling in a strange way, like she did sometimes when Courtney had to get a shot at the doctor's office. It was a smile meant to be reassuring, but it betrayed a bit of anxiousness. Courtney felt her heart beat a little faster.

Her mother stroked Courtney's fine, tawny hair and continued. "Remember when I went to the interview in Washington a few months back? Well, I got the job. I'll be leading a whole team of other nurses and helping to train new ones. It's what I've been working toward for years, to make a better life for us."

Her mother paused, rubbed her hands together, and looked at Courtney, who felt confused. She wanted to say, *But we live here. How will you work in Washington?* But the words didn't seem to come.

"The thing is…." Her mother's grey-blue eyes looked at her with concern. "Well, honey, we'll have to move… to Washington, DC."

Courtney furrowed her brow. She felt like she was waiting for the punch line, as if her mother had just told her a joke. "But what about Gran and Grandpap, and my friends, and school?" she said in a rush, feeling dizzy.

She had forgotten about the job in Washington. When her mother had gone to the interview, Courtney barely gave it a second thought. It had not occurred to her that it was a real, possible thing and that they might have to move. To her, it was like her mother had just taken a short trip. Courtney even got a souvenir, a small model of the White House.

Now questions swirled in her head. How could they leave her grandparents and her friends? It was just the two of them. Who would help with her math homework if her grandpap wasn't there? Who would take care of her after school? How could she leave Jane and Eric?

"We'll visit here a lot," her mother said. "You will start at a new school and make new friends. I know it seems like we'll be leaving a lot behind, but I really think it's the best decision. I want you to experience the city now that you're older. It will be fun."

"But I don't want to start a new school. I want to stay here. I don't care about the city. I like it here," Courtney protested. She hadn't meant to, but warm tears began to trickle down her cheeks.

Her mom tried to hold her hand, but she pulled it back. "Listen," her mom began, "it's never easy to leave what you know and put yourself in a new place, but we can do it. And Uncle Tim and Aunt Kelly will be nearby. We'll have them."

"I don't care about your stupid job. I don't want to leave!" Courtney was crying loudly, letting the tears drip down her face. Some pieces of hair clung like wet mop strings to her cheeks, but she didn't try to push them away.

"Please don't be so upset," her mom stood and bent to hug her. "Let me get you a tissue."

Then, before she knew what she was doing, Courtney walked out the back door and around to the front yard, where she hopped on her bike and was gone before her mother returned to the kitchen.

* * *

Dusk was just beginning to settle. The crickets were growing louder, filling the air around her until Courtney began to worry she might not hear the cars. She pedaled fast up Penmar Road, breathing hard, thankful that the wind was drying her tear-muddled cheeks. She passed Mr. Garrison's orchards, which were almost fully in bloom. She could smell apples and peaches and earth, a heavy scent in the dry heat of late July. She passed the cows lying around at Kepler's dairy farm, tired after the evening milking. She realized she might miss even the pungent smell of manure that was impossible to avoid passing by here.

She stopped at the yellow brick house on the corner, her grandparents' home. Courtney adored the house: the tall, skinny windows and the big, old wooden front porch where she'd spent hours reading and playing games with Jane and Eric. Staring at it now, it was the first time she had ever experienced the feeling of missing something before leaving it.

When her mother arrived a few minutes later, Courtney was sitting with her grandparents in the living room.

"Courtney, you know better than to run off like that!" her mother said with a raised voice.

When Courtney began to tear up, her mother's anger faded. She sat beside her on the sofa. "Just don't do it again. I know you're upset, but we can talk through it."

Courtney nodded. She wanted to say she was sorry, that she hadn't meant to leave; it just kind of happened. She looked at her hands in her lap.

Instead of staying for the tea and cookies Gran offered, Courtney's mom said they'd better get going. They walked to the car without a word. The sky blazed bright pink above the orchards and the low mountains that nestled the town.

"I'm sorry," her mother said in the car. "I know you don't want to go, but I really think it will be good for us.

Don't you want to explore the city, see the monuments and buildings, the big zoo? You can play soccer and try rowing if you want. There are lots of rivers. We'll see Gran and Grandpap very often. It will be all right, I promise."

Courtney didn't feel like saying anything, but she heard sadness in her mother's voice and felt guilty about her earlier getaway. "Mama, do they have farms in Washington? What if I don't find a best friend?"

Her mother sighed and put her arm around Courtney. "Oh, honey, you can email and phone Jane and Eric all you want. And I don't think there are farms in the city, but there are some around. Remember, it's not too far from here. We will visit a lot, okay?"

When Courtney didn't reply, her mother said, "Listen, I'll make a deal with you: let's try Washington, and if you really aren't happy, we can make another change, all right?"

"Like, come back to Waynesboro?" Courtney asked.

"Yes," her mom answered.

"Okay. Thank you, Mama."

"You're welcome, dove."

When they got home, her mother showed her on the computer their new neighborhood and some of the interesting things they could do there. She showed her how close they'd be to Uncle Tim and Aunt Kelly, whom Courtney loved. She felt a little ripple of excitement and relief that her mother had promised to return if Courtney was unhappy.

For a long while before she fell asleep, Courtney watched the great maple tree outside her window, its shadowy branches shivering in the moonlight. She imagined Washington and wondered if she would ever love it as much as Waynesboro. She felt like she could give it a try.

The Missing Fox Fur

by Sarah Marino
illustrated by Dion Williams

It seemed that Great Aunt Rose's fox fur was missing. I had just walked in the door from my friend's house across the street, and my mother was on the phone. I decided to wait by the stairs before going up to my room. If there were any details my mother was willing to share, I had to be there to get them.

"I'll check around the house, Rose. Mm-hmm," my mother said. "No, as far as I know, Ian is not on drugs, nor is he a thief. I will talk to you later. Goodbye."

I heard Mom click the phone button to hang up, so I went into the kitchen. She made a groaning noise and clenched her hand around the cordless, then pushed it away on the countertop.

"Mom?" I asked.

"Oh, hi, Katie. I didn't hear you come in." Her eyes looked tired behind her glasses, and her voice sounded quieter than usual. "That was Great Aunt Rose. It seems her fur coat has been taken and she's very concerned."

"She thinks Ian took it?" I asked.

"Yes, unfortunately. The kid becomes a vegetarian and the world suspects him of the worst," my mother said, smiling. "Although...you don't happen to know anything, do you?" Her smile disappeared.

In fact, I did know a little bit, but I wasn't sure whether or not I should share. Yes, Ian was my older brother, and yes, he often teased me and did gross things, like put stink bugs in my bed to freak me out. But he also did great things, like take me around the campus at the University of Chicago and treat me to lunch where they served greasy, delicious pizza. Doing these things with an older brother when you yourself were only thirteen, well, it was really cool, not to mention impressive to

41

other kids in my class (although I knew not to be too much of a showoff about such things).

Earlier that week, Ian told me that he and Prema were going to a demonstration for PETA and he asked if I wanted to go. I wasn't entirely sure what a demonstration was or what PETA did. Ian had tried to explain, telling me that PETA stood for People for the Ethical Treatment of Animals. I was totally for treating animals ethically, but I declined. I was kind of shy around Prema and definitely felt too shy to attend a demonstration. Plus, the demonstration had something to do with the fact that Ian no longer ate meat. Ian had changed a lot since becoming Prema's boyfriend. The biggest noticeable change was, of course, the no-meat thing. Ian used to be a connoisseur of burgers, making the entire family go to new restaurants to test recipes he'd found online.

Would I be betraying my brother by telling Mom about the demonstration? I mean, I didn't know much about it, other than it was happening and he had planned to attend. He certainly hadn't mentioned stealing Aunt Rose's coat.

"Katie, I know you care about your brother, but could you tell me if you know anything?" Mom stared at me, pleading. I was a horrible liar. I accidentally started biting my nails, and then it was over. "Katie, I just need to know."

I sighed. "He told me that he and Prema were going to a PETA demonstration, but that's all he said. I don't know where it is or anything else."

"PETA? They're that serious about this?" Mom asked. She paced around the kitchen. "Well, I'm not going to presume guilt. Heaven knows Aunt Rose doesn't really need that coat. She only wears it to church on the coldest of days," Mom laughed. I chuckled, unaware of whether she actually saw any humor in the situation or was only trying to relieve stress. "If he did take it," she continued, "he'll have to make amends. It's completely unacceptable to take anyone else's property. You know that, right, Katherine?"

"Yes, Mom, I know."

"Good. Why don't you go start your homework? I need to call your father." Mom stepped into the living room and started dialing.

I went to my room and, after a moment's hesitation, sent a text to Ian:

Sorry, I had to mention the PETA thing. Do you know about Aunt Rose's coat? Mom is suspicious.

In the quiet of my room, after I had put my things away, I realized I didn't want to do homework and wished I had told Ian I would go to the demonstration. I sat on my bed and texted again:

Is it too late for me to meet you?

The cool thing (and the terrible thing) about having an older sibling is that you always wish you were where they were. Whatever stage of life they were at, it always seemed infinitely cooler than where you were. I was cursed with this longing. I wanted to be through high school, in college. Ian told me to be patient, that I would have all of that in due time, that I should enjoy it as it unfolded. In the meantime, I could experience it through his eyes sometimes.

I was about to turn on some music when I got a text:

Ugh, Mom, Aunt Rose. It's OK. I was going to confess anyway. It's still going on. Walk down to Union and Hyde.

I smiled, interpreting "I was going to confess anyway" to mean "I did take Aunt Rose's coat." Then I realized he'd again made me part of his scheme by telling me. I was kind of an accomplice now; I had even more information to try to *not* share with Mom.

I decided the best thing to do would be to leave the house. Avoidance is sometimes the best remedy.

I was used to going to campus on my own, because my father teaches in the Fine Art department at the U of Chicago and Ian is now a freshman there. Ian is really smart, another thing that makes me both love him and strongly dislike him (or rather, envy him with a passion). He is only seventeen, but he was able to skip his last year of high school to start college because he'd won some science competition.

I went downstairs and Mom was reading in the living room. "I'm taking a walk," I said as I opened the door, hoping to avoid a conversation.

"Okay, see you in a while." She barely glanced at me. I was free.

It was a warm spring day, and the sky was blue with small puffy clouds. It was almost five o'clock. We lived on a pretty, busy street near the university. There were old houses, apartment buildings, wide sidewalks, a school, an old Catholic church, a laundromat, a convenience store, and several restaurants. There was always something or someone to notice. Today, though, I was hurrying.

I could hear the bullhorn a few blocks away from the intersection Ian had mentioned. As I neared the corner, I saw something curious: a fur coat on a t-shaped contraption was raised above people's heads, with a sign on the front of the coat reading "NO MORE FUR." It looked a lot like Aunt Rose's coat. It was such an odd, surprising sight that I couldn't help but laugh.

There were about forty people standing in a group. Most of them looked to be about Ian's age, but a few had grayish hair. Two women were pushing strollers with toddlers. One man with dark hair pulled into a ponytail stood on a makeshift platform and shouted every so often into the bullhorn. He was yelling several different messages: "End cruelty to animals," "Fur isn't fair," "Factory farms pollute and kill," and "Everyone is an animal; stop animal cruelty!" I stood across the street, feeling self-conscious and confused. No one was really paying attention to me, though.

"Hey, you made it. Come on, Prema is over there," Ian said, startling me.

"Ian, is that..." I hesitated, looking over at the raised fur coat.

He smiled. "Yes, it is. Did she really need it?"

"You didn't have to steal it," I said, following him across the street.

"Calm down, Kate. I'll take the heat for it. Don't you think her coat is serving a better purpose here, where it might help prevent other foxes from being killed, instead of in her closet?"

I couldn't argue with that one. It was hard to argue with an older, collegiate brother about an issue I had never pondered until he kind of forced it into my life. I felt overwhelmed and noticed I was sweating a little bit.

Another one of the more annoying ways in which Ian had changed recently was his sudden talkativeness. Every time I saw him now, he was talking about Prema and trying to convert me to vegetarianism and describing how animals lived on farms, all crowded together. He would describe how they keep them in farms to make fur coats out of them, saying it isn't like Grandpa's days of hunting. The animals aren't free anymore and they die slowly, and often painfully. Part of me was interested and I did stop eating as much meat, but I was only thirteen, and sometimes I had to eat what was on my plate.

"Hi, Kate," Prema said. "I'm glad you came." Her black hair was braided and pulled to one side. She wore jeans and a long-sleeved shirt that had a bunny and the phrase "No Chemical Testing, Please."

"Hi," I replied.

"Here, take a sign," Ian said, thrusting a large signpost into my hands. It said "Ban Puppy Mills" and had a picture of an adorable puppy that made me sad and happy all at once. The sign was heavy. The group had started walking in a circle, and although we were on the outside, I started to feel dizzy watching them. They were chanting in unison. Ian tried to push me into the circle with him and Prema, but I moved aside, feeling dizzier. He followed me.

"I'm sorry," I said, feeling like I might cry. "I, I think I just wanted to watch."

"I understand. I shouldn't have pushed you in." Ian put his arm around my shoulders.

"Actually," I said, "I'm worried about the coat and telling Mom and Dad. I don't want to lie for you."

"I don't want you to lie for me. I'll tell them."

"Could you tell them now?" I asked. Ian agreed to come back to the house with me if I could just wait a little longer for the demonstration to wind down. I agreed. I found a space and stood, still holding the sign and listening to the chorus of chanting voices. Many of the cars driving by beeped excitedly to show support. Eventually I felt less overwhelmed and started to have a pretty good time.

* * *

"Do you think they'll make me tell Aunt Rose in person? Or repay her?" Ian asked. The group had dispersed and we were walking home.

"You stole her coat, Ian. Reality check," Prema pointed out. Then she added quickly, "Although, it was a noble thing to do." She linked her arm in his and cuddled him.

We got to the house and were hit with parental disapproval as soon we stepped into the living room. "Ian, what's this about a PETA demonstration and Aunt Rose's coat?" my father asked.

"We don't want to assume you took it, but did you take it?" Mom asked.

Ian nodded. My parents erupted with exasperated moans and sighs.

"I understand your motives, and I admire your devotion to this issue, but it is not acceptable to take someone else's possessions. We taught you better than that," Dad said. His voice was more disappointed than angry, but it sounded so sad that I wished it were the other way around.

"I'm sorry. I know it was wrong," Ian said. "She didn't need the coat, though. Do I have to tell her I took it?"

"Ian, you've really put us in a tough situation," Mom said. "We feel that you need to admit what you did, but at the same time, we're aware of how awkward that would be, for all future family get-togethers, not to mention the heartache it would cause your aunt when she realizes that her dear great-nephew is a thief."

"But, Mom, you said earlier that Aunt Rose didn't need the coat! Ian is sorry. And fur coats are bad!" I shouted. Everyone turned and looked at me.

My mother's eyes widened. "Katherine, thank you for your opinion. I'm glad you've gotten your sister into it too, Ian." She seemed to hiss the words out.

"Tina, take a breath. Let's not let our frustration get the best of us," Dad said. Mom sighed and sat down. "Ian, it's not your beliefs we're angry about. You have a right to believe what you want. It's the fact that you stole someone else's property. You understand that, right?"

Ian nodded.

"In the interest of protecting Aunt Rose's feelings and the peace of future family gatherings, I think we should *not* tell Rose that you took the coat. However, you will pay to replace the coat, to buy her another one. I suspect she knows you took it since there was no evidence of forced entry and you were just there mowing her lawn. But I think it would only hurt her more to tell her definitively that you did take it." Dad walked over to Ian and put his arm around him.

"I'm sorry, Dad."

"Once you take one thing, it might seem okay to do it again. You might think the consequences won't be so bad." Dad took a step away from Ian and added, "I'm asking you, son, please don't do anything like this again. Use other methods to advance your cause."

No one said anything for a minute that felt like an hour. Then Prema started sniffling.

"I've never heard someone's parent say something so kind," she said. "My father would never…" Her voice stopped. Ian wrapped her in his arms.

"Thanks, Dad, and Mom," Ian said, leading Prema outside.

I sat down on the couch and Dad sat next to me. "So, are we going to be making meatless meatballs now?"

I rolled my eyes. "Maybe. I don't understand it all, but I definitely don't ever want a fur coat."

"You can do what you feel is best, Kate. You're a good kid," Mom said, coming over to hug me.

As much as I liked being told I was a good kid, I wanted to talk to one of my own friends. I excused myself and went outside. As I walked down the front steps, I could see Ian and Prema kissing in front of a house down the block. I looked away, feeling embarrassed, but they didn't see me. I was kind of envious and disgusted all at once. I wondered what kissing felt like. I thought about what Prema had said about her dad. Even though I wasn't sure what she'd meant, I felt sad for her and glad that she had Ian.

I realized how much I'd seen that day. I was beginning to see how I could enjoy the time as it unfolded, as Ian had said. I could become a vegetarian or not; I could demonstrate or not; I could know about kissing when the time came. The choices seemed endless, and I was excited to start making them.

The Flag of McHenry

by Michael Scotto
illustrated by Dion Williams

Some called it the War of 1812, for the year it began. But as that year ended, and the fighting dragged on, people began to call it the "Second War for Independence." No matter the label, the conflict remained the same. For the second time in its history, America was at war with the British Empire. And the British were winning.

By the fall season of 1814, that fact was crystal clear. In late August, the Redcoats seized Washington. They destroyed many government buildings. They even burned the President's House. The following month, the British chose their next target: the city of Baltimore. It was America's third-largest city, and a major hub for trade. If the British took Baltimore, they could break America's morale and win the war. Only one defense stood in their way. It was called Fort McHenry, a star-shaped stronghold that stood on the harbor's edge.

As dawn lit on September 13, British warships sailed into the Chesapeake Bay. Armed with cannons, bombs, and rockets, the British were determined to do their worst. The bay waters churned as the warships approached. The sailors on deck loaded their guns. Within Fort McHenry, American soldiers steeled themselves. No one knew if the fort could withstand the British attack. As the warships drew closer, more than a few men said their prayers.

But this is not a story about soldiers. The battle and their bravery are very important—and certainly worth recounting. But this particular story is not theirs. This is the story of an elderly doctor and the two young men who saved his life.

As the British warships entered the harbor, one ship stayed behind. It was not a British ship. It was an American vessel called the *Minden*. The *Minden* was anchored far away from the fort, about eight miles off the coast. Aboard its deck, Dr. William Beanes and his two saviors waited. It was all they could do.

Dr. Beanes, a gentleman of sixty-five, rested his weary bones upon a crate. From time to time, he absently reached for his nose, to touch the spot where his spectacles usually lay.

How could you have forgotten them? Beanes cursed himself.

In fairness, the doctor had not simply forgotten his glasses. Two weeks earlier, British soldiers had burst into his room in the dead of the night. The Redcoats dragged him from bed and took him out to sea as their prisoner. They had not allowed him to bring anything along, save the bedclothes he had been wearing.

However, Beanes was not in an especially fair mood. He was tired, angry, and afraid. *And blind as a mole,* he lamented. The old man closed his eyes. The *Minden* swayed on the waves beneath him. Its gentle rocking soothed his heart.

Beanes opened his eyes and looked toward his rescuers, two young lawyers. Before they had come, Beanes had been certain that he would be killed. Instead, these brave men, these strangers, had sailed out to the British fleet and negotiated for his life. After several days of talk, they had convinced a top general to allow Beanes's release—but on one condition. The three men could not return to shore until after the battle in Baltimore was through.

And so they waited. Beanes watched one of the lawyers pace by him. It was the younger of the two, Mr. Skinner. He was marching the ship's deck from bow to stern. The other lawyer sat quietly in a corner of the deck. His name was Francis Key. Where Skinner was all nerves, Mr. Key seemed completely serene. He was writing on a scrap of paper, calm as a pastor on Sunday afternoon.

Key glanced up from his writing. "Take care, Mr. Skinner," he said. "You'll tread a hole in the deck and fall into our sleeping quarters."

Skinner stopped, a bit embarrassed. "Yes, yes," he said, distracted. "Fine point." Beanes watched him lean against the ship's mast. After a moment, though, Skinner's foot set to tapping. Within a minute, he was on the march once again.

Francis Key leaned toward Dr. Beanes. "It seems that he is irredeemable," he confided with a smile.

"You might be right, lad," replied Beanes. His family had lived in Maryland for generations, but his voice still bore a bit of a Scottish accent. "Mr. Key, might I ask what you are writing?"

"This?" asked Key, holding up his scrap of paper. His cheeks flushed slightly red, as if he were embarrassed. "I dabble a bit in poetry. It isn't very good, mind you. It does seem to settle my mind, though."

Beanes nodded, and he rubbed at the bridge of his nose. "Ah, blast it," he muttered.

Key placed his quill pen in the inkwell by his feet. "Are you quite all right, Doctor?" he asked.

"My spectacles," groused Beanes. "I can barely see beyond the tip of my nose without them. If you could oblige me—what do you see out yonder?"

Key stood and faced the shore. He peered through a hand-held telescope that he had borrowed from a sailor. "The warships are in formation," he said. "It should not be long before the first shots are fired."

"What of McHenry?" asked Beanes. "Do you think they are prepared?"

Key squinted. "The men are too small to see," he replied. "But I can see their flag, flying high. I can see every star and every stripe, sure as the sun rose."

"You can see all that?" inquired Beanes. "It must be quite a banner."

Skinner stepped up beside Beanes and Key. "Thirty feet tall, forty-two feet wide," he said proudly.

Beanes looked quizzically at Skinner.

"It's rather famous in fair Baltimore," Skinner explained. "Fort McHenry's commander had it made specially. He told the seamstress that he wanted those Redcoats to be certain of where they could find him."

Beanes, Key, and Skinner laughed together. After a few seconds, though, a British cannon shot off with a roar. The men fell silent as the cannonball soared toward Fort McHenry and landed with a powerful explosion. Beanes could not see where it landed, but did he not need to. He needed only to look at Key and Skinner's shocked faces.

Key looked at Beanes, trying to hide his dismay. "All will be well, friend," he said. "As long as that flag flies, we can be sure that the fort has held."

The other ships joined in the attack. All through the morning, they peppered Fort McHenry with cannonballs, exploding bombs, and even rockets.

It was almost too much for Dr. Beanes to bear. Looking out, he could see the red flames of the soaring British rockets. The exploding bombs flashed as blurs in the distance. But he could not see the damage when they landed. He could only imagine it. He thought of the men in the fort and wondered how many needed a doctor's help.

"What can you see, lads?" asked Beanes frantically. "Is the flag still there?"

"The flag still flies," replied Mr. Key.

The warships rained down destruction all afternoon and into the evening. As Skinner paced about, Key described the scene to Beanes as best as he could. Mortar bombs burst over the fort like fireworks, spraying it with flame and metal shards. The fort walls were charred, even crumbling in some places. "But the flag still flies," Key always added.

Soon, darkness fell. The smoky cannon fire blocked out the moon, and the only light came from rockets and exploding bombs. Beanes, Key, and Skinner watched it well into the night.

The doctor grasped his silver hair in anguish. "How could anything survive this torrent?" he asked. "What could remain?"

He watched Key lift his telescope to his eye. Flashes of red light lit across the lawyer's smooth face. "The smoke is too thick to tell," he said.

Hours passed, each seeming slower than the last. Red and white danced across the ship's deck, across Beanes's trembling hands. Then, as suddenly as the battle had begun, the cannon fire ceased.

"What's happened?" asked Beanes in the darkness.

"The battle is through," replied Skinner.

"Can you see anything, Mr. Key?" he asked. "Does McHenry's banner still fly?"

Beanes felt Key's hand grab his shoulder. "We will have to wait 'til morning," the lawyer answered.

The *Minden* rocked in the silent sea. To Beanes, the quiet was almost more painful than the battle. He did not sleep a wink.

Eventually, the sun peeked up over the city of Baltimore. As dawn rose on September 14, Beanes gazed toward the fort. He saw that Key was awake as well. "Please," he implored, "tell me what you see."

Key raised his telescope and looked one last time. He quietly lowered it back to his side. Beanes and Skinner waited. "Well?" asked Skinner.

Key turned to face the men. Tears glinted in his eyes. "The banner waves," he said.

The fort had survived! Skinner erupted in a cheer.

"It is tattered and torn," Key told Beanes, "but it still waves." Beanes's lips spread into a smile.

Skinner paced up the deck and down, shouting for joy.

"Always on the march," Beanes remarked with a grin.

Suddenly, Key seemed to join Skinner in his rushing.

"Not you, too!" cried Beanes. He sat on a crate. "I'll not be joining you prancing lads."

"No, I need my quill, my ink!" exclaimed Key. He hunched over as he walked, searching the floor. "Oh, I hope I did not kick them over in the dark."

Beanes reached behind his crate and produced Key's writing tools. "Here, lad," he said. "I set them aside for you."

Key took the quill and inkwell from Beanes. "Oh, thank you, Doctor!" he said. "I have something I must write down."

That morning, the *Minden* returned to the Chesapeake Bay. Ashore, Dr. Beanes thanked Mr. Key and Skinner, and they went their separate ways. Key returned to Washington, and Dr. Beanes to his farm outside of Baltimore. Though the doctor was a bit of a celebrity in his town, his life largely continued unchanged. He did, however, make a habit of carrying his spectacles to bed with him.

Weeks passed. Beanes treated patients and read the newspaper for stories about the war. The battle at Fort McHenry had been a turning point. The Americans had renewed confidence. For example, the President's House was already under repair. The builders were painting it white to hide the burn marks.

One day in late fall, Beanes discovered a piece of writing with a very familiar author. On the newspaper's second page, Beanes found a poem written by one Francis Scott Key, Washington lawyer. An article accompanied it. Beanes read that the poem had been inspired by the attack on Fort McHenry. It had already been performed at a theater in Washington to great success.

The poem was set to the tune of a popular song that the doctor happened to know. Beanes decided to sing the poem aloud. He removed his spectacles so that he could read the tiny print. He cleared his throat, and sang:

O! say can you see by the dawn's early light,
What so proudly we hailed at the twilight's last gleaming,
Whose broad stripes and bright stars, through the perilous fight,
O'er the ramparts we watch'd, were so gallantly streaming?
And the Rockets' red glare, the Bombs bursting in air,
Gave proof through the night that our Flag was still there;
O! say does that star-spangled banner yet wave,
O'er the Land of the free, and the home of the brave?

The doctor lowered the paper, a lump in his throat. The memories of that whole day aboard the *Minden* flooded his mind. The thunderous explosions, the streaks in the sky, the fear, the panic—they overcame him in a rush. But old William Beanes pictured one thing most clear. It was Key's face at dawn, his tears of pride and wonder, when he spotted the triumphant flag.

Author's Note

While the dialogue in this story is invented, the events described in the story are true, and the characters featured are real. Francis Scott Key really did witness the assault on Fort McHenry from aboard a ship in the Chesapeake Bay. As described in this account, Mr. Key, a lawyer, had come to negotiate the release of a doctor who had been captured by the British Army. After watching the battle, where the Americans succeeded in holding the British back, Key was inspired to write the poem that is now the national anthem of the United States.

Steven and the Turtles

by Summer Swauger
illustrated by Mallory Chick

October 5, 2011

Commissioner Henry Parnell
Massachusetts Department of Environmental Protection
One Winter Street
Boston, Massachusetts 02108

Dear Commissioner Parnell,

My name is Steven Brown, and I am a fourth grader at Hillsboro Elementary School. I am writing to you because yesterday I found pollution near the forest by my house. Pollution is very bad for the environment, plants, animals, and people. I learned in science class that all living things depend on clean air to breathe and clean water to drink. But pollution makes the air and water dirty. I am afraid that the pollution I found will destroy my favorite part of the forest. It could make the plants and animals sick. I need your help!

My family lives on a small farm at the edge of Myles Standish State Forest in Plymouth County, Massachusetts. I like to explore the forest looking for cool plants and animals. I don't go too far when I'm by myself, though, because I'm not allowed. Yesterday after school, my mom said that I could walk down to the pond. It is right inside the forest. The pond is my favorite place to go because there are turtles living near it. I like to watch them swim in the water and lie in the sun.

But when I got to the pond, I noticed a weird smell. It smelled like the stuff my mom uses to mop the floor. I didn't know where it was coming from. After looking around for a while, I didn't see anything near the pond, so I walked farther along the forest edge. I passed the line where our property ends and the next farm begins. This farm has been abandoned for as long as I can remember. I climbed the steep hill leading up to where the old farmhouse used to be. I thought I might be able to get a better look into the forest from high up. But as I climbed the hill, the smell got stronger. Soon it was stinging my nose. At the top of the hill, I couldn't believe what I saw! There were all these barrels lying on their sides, and there was green liquid everywhere. And the smell was awful! Someone must have dumped those barrels on the abandoned farmland, thinking that no one would find them.

I knew right away that this was pollution because we are learning about it in school. My teacher Mrs. Jones said that pollution is very harmful to the plants and animals living in an area. She also said that it is our job to take care of the environment and all living things. I was very angry. Who could do such a terrible thing?

Suddenly, I remembered the turtles that live near the pond. If those smelly chemicals leaked down the hill into the forest, the turtles could die! I had looked those turtles up on the Internet a few days before. They were Plymouth red-bellied turtles. They are on the endangered species list! They only live here in Massachusetts and in a few other New England states. In fact, there are only about three hundred of those turtles on the whole earth! I knew I had to rescue the turtles before they got sick, but I was afraid I might already be too late.

I ran back down the hill into the forest. Then all of a sudden, I heard a quad driving by. It was a park ranger! So I ran over, waving my arms and yelling for him to stop. The park ranger said his name was Josh and asked me what was wrong.

So I told Josh about the barrels leaking the gooey green chemicals on the abandoned farm. I said that I was afraid the chemicals might leak into the forest. Then I explained that I knew the turtles living near the pond were Plymouth red-bellied turtles, an endangered species. Josh asked me to show him where I found the barrels. I took him out of the forest and up the hill. When he saw the mess, he looked very sad and very angry. He was just as angry as I was! He promised to report the chemical spill immediately and that he would take care of the turtles and all the other wildlife that lived near the forest edge. Then he told me to go home because he didn't want me to get sick from the chemical fumes.

When I got home, I told my mom about how someone had dumped chemicals up on the hill on the abandoned farm. I was very sad to think that the turtles and the other plants and animals in the forest could die because someone had polluted the area. I was also sad because I felt like there was nothing I could do to help. My mom suggested that I write a letter to the Massachusetts Department of Environmental Protection. She said that the organization works to protect wildlife in our area. That's why I'm writing to you. I am hoping that since you are the commissioner, this letter will convince you and your organization to save the turtles and other living things in the forest by helping to clean up the chemical spill.

It is bad enough that the chemicals polluted the land on the farm. But if the harmful chemicals run down the hill from the farm and into the forest, all the living things near the forest edge would be lost. The smell from the chemicals could drive the animals away or make them sick. If it rains, the rain might wash the chemicals down the hill and into the pond. If any animals drink the toxic water, they will die. The chemicals might also get into the dirt in the forest, killing the trees that some animals live in and the plants they eat. I am especially worried about the turtles because if the chemicals hurt them, the species will be even closer to extinction. Please save the turtles and the other wildlife in the forest.

I am also asking you to make sure that no one else can dump chemicals near Myles Standish State Forest. You should ask the Massachusetts government to hire more park rangers like Josh to patrol near the edges of the forest. You should also ask the government to make stricter laws against pollution. The stricter laws might make someone think twice before polluting the environment. Last, you should give educational classes at the Plymouth Community Center to teach people that littering and dumping chemicals is bad. Maybe if more people knew how bad pollution is for the earth, not as many people would do it. Please help to keep the forest and the earth clean for all living things.

Sincerely,

Steven Brown

Letters from a Young Gold Miner

by Michael Scotto
illustrated by Sean Kennedy

May 10, 1849

Dear Mrs. Atwood,

I apologize for taking so long to write. This has been my first chance to send any letters since I left. I hope that I have not caused you or Mr. Atwood any worry.

I cannot believe that it has been two months since I set sail! My ship arrived in San Francisco yesterday morning. What a strange little city! The locals call it the "City of Dust" because of the dust in the wind and the gold dust in everyone's pockets.

I write to you from the King's Hotel, which is not as elegant as you might reckon. In truth, it is little more than a cabin with cloth sheets for walls. Even so, you would not believe the expense for a night's boarding. The cost of everything out West is much dearer than at home. A pound of potatoes, which costs a half-penny in Boston, runs for one dollar out here. Can you imagine?

Anyhow, I should not complain. Tomorrow morning, I will buy a pick for excavating and ride off for gold country! I am too excited to sleep. I can recall every story told by the men in Mr. Atwood's barbershop.

I do hope that Mr. Atwood is getting along well without me. He is not still cross with me, is he? I have said so on many a day, but please remind him that I verily enjoyed being his apprentice. However, when the "gold fever" came about…well, I had to see the elephant, as they say. I am sure that you have already found a good replacement who can sweep the cut hair, strop the razors, and lather the shave water.

I still have the gift Mr. Atwood left for me—the shaving kit. I found it atop my suitcase just before I left. Please tell him that I will cherish it for all my days…even if I cannot yet grow the beard to use it. The razor's pearl handle is beautiful.

It should be about four days' ride to the foot of the Sierra Mountains. With luck, I will make it to a mining camp in time to celebrate my sixteenth birthday. Perhaps I will find a rich vein of gold. What a birthday gift that would be!

I will write again once I reach camp. By the way—how do you like my penmanship? Though I could not send letters at sea, I practiced my writing just as you instructed me. I hope that it shows, ma'am.

Kindest wishes,

Rupert Slade

May 17, 1849

Dear Mrs. Atwood,

I arrived yesterday afternoon at the mining camp. As you can see, I did not make it in time to enjoy my birthday here. Still, the family I rode out with gave me an extra helping of mutton and bread tea, which I enjoyed heartily. It is good to find people with souls as kind as yours and Mr. Atwood's, especially in such an alien place.

Not everyone is so kind and fair. I learned that in dealing with the mining supplier. It happened the morning I was to leave San Francisco. I had spent all but my last three dollars on lodging at the King's, and I still needed to buy a mining pick. The supplier, though, refused to sell me one for less than seven dollars! Finally, he agreed to sell me the pick at a lay of three dollars, plus my wide-brim hat. The hat only cost twenty cents, so I thought it quite agreeable. Only when I arrived yesterday did I realize that the no-account plunderer had left me at the little end of the horn. My pick's handle was cracked plum up the middle. It was as useless as teeth on a chicken!

Fortunately, my camp straddles the American River, so I can just pan for gold in the water. The tin lather bowl from my shaving kit will be of great use for that. (Please do not tell Mr. Atwood about this.)

The name of my camp is rather gruesome; they call it Stretch Neck Gulch. It got its name on account of the local *alcalde*. That is a Spanish word which means "judge." In the camp's early days, two miners were caught stealing, and the *alcalde* ruled that they should be hanged for their deed. It might seem overly harsh, but I have grown glad that such things are treated so seriously. Many other camps have mighty problems with crime, so I've heard.

Stretch Neck is a wondrous place. It seems like all creation has come to California. In a single day's time, I have spotted whites working alongside men of color, and men from China, France, Ireland, and England, all mining full chisel. For all the variety of men, though, there are no ladies at camp. I suppose that is why all of the men have allowed their hair to grow so long and their beards so unkempt. If only Mr. Atwood could see it! He would be quite amused—or perhaps disgusted, I cannot be certain which.

Anyhow, the sun has risen, and so I must snuff my candle and make way to my claim. A "claim" is the patch of land where each miner hunts for gold. I will write again at my nearest opportunity. The express comes through weekly to gather letters, so you will likely hear from me then. Wish me luck!

All my best,

Rupert Slade

June 11, 1849

Dear Mrs. Atwood,

I apologize for not writing as promised. Panning in the river is more wearying than I would ever have guessed. The fiery sun has fried the nape of my neck like a strip of bacon. (Oh, how I wish I had not traded away my hat!) The river water, in contrast, is as cold as a snow bank. As I pan each day, it turns my hands and feet nearly to ice blocks. How the sun can burn so brightly and the water remain so chilly, I will never understand. These are the conditions in which we toil from dawn until candle-lighting, with nary a break between.

At my claim, I have one good neighbor and one poor one. My good neighbor has the claim directly behind mine. He is a Texan with a narrow face and a booming laugh. My other neighbor works a claim in front of me. He is a nasty colossus of a man, with a dirty, wooly beard and cruel, blue eyes. In my thoughts I call him the Ogre, because he reminds me of a giant from a fairy tale.

I must confess, Mr. Atwood was right. Panning is not nearly as romantic as the men at the barbershop described it. It is terribly tedious work. Over and over, I dip my lather bowl into the water, scraping it along the riverbed. I haul out a scoop of rocks and dirty water, and then I have to swirl it. The swirling reveals any gold that is hidden in the rocks and dirt. Thus far, though, I have not seen the effect often. I have yet to find more than a few pebbles of gold. It has been enough to buy food, but only barely.

Anyhow, all this is the reason I have not written. By each day's end I find myself, as my neighbor the Texan put it, "catawamptiously chewed up." That is a Southern way of saying "very tired." It is an accurate phrase—simply writing it is exhausting.

As the weeks wear on, I will be more judicious in writing. It raises my spirit to share with you my adventures. I hope that you are pleased to receive them.

Good health and warmest regards,

Rupert Slade

June 18, 1849

Dear Mrs. Atwood,

I hope this letter finds you well. I do not have much in the way of news, but I feel a fierce urge to write.

For a place so cluttered, Stretch Neck Gulch can be quite lonesome. After dusk, the other men spend their leisure time (and their earnings) on gambling and drink. I often pass my nights alone in my tent. During the day, the Texan teaches me songs to sing as I pan for gold. Sadly, ma'am, the songs only bring to mind the piano in your parlor and how beautifully you would play and sing.

Worst of all, though, is my rotten neighbor, the Ogre. He has developed a foul habit of spitting his dipping tobacco into my piece of the river. I am afraid to speak up, even to the Texan, for fear that the brute will overhear me and smite me over the head.

I miss Boston terribly. I miss the laughter of the barbershop and the taste of your Sunday oyster stew. I even miss Mr. Atwood's barbering lessons. It would please me very much to hear from the both of you…but I do not know how you would reach me.

Your solitary friend,

Rupert Slade

July 9, 1849

Dear Mr. and Mrs. Atwood,

I must start, once again, with an apology. I have again been careless about corresponding, and have let several weeks slip by without a word. But once you learn of my circumstances, you will doubtless understand what has kept me away.

Shortly after I sent off my previous letter, I returned to my claim. After about an hour of scooping and swirling, I finally hit a stroke of luck: pay dirt! That is what we call a scoop that bears gold. This was no pebble that I found— it was a nugget the size of my fist! I instantly turned back to my friend the Texan and cried out, "Eureka!"

The Texan was sloshing through the river to congratulate me, when I felt a heavy hand on my shoulder. It was the Ogre. He spun me around and demanded that I hand him the gold nugget. He said that I did not get it from my claim, but rather, I stole it from his! We began to argue quite heatedly. For your sake, Mrs. Atwood, I will not recount exactly what language I used.

The giant and I carried on all possessed-like until finally, he seized my arms and threw me down into the stream. I stumbled in the rocks and my ankle wrenched with a pop. The Ogre, laughing, snatched up my gold nugget and lumbered off to the saloon.

I begged the Texan to help me. The Ogre was a thief, and I wanted to find our *alcalde*—the judge, you recall. You will never guess what the Texan told me. That beast, the Ogre…he was the *alcalde*! I was dumbstruck.

The Texan did help me, though, over to the camp doctor's tent. The doctor, with his shaggy beard, looked scarcely different from the miners. His white coat had long been browned by dust. He told me that my anklebone was broken, and I would not be able to pan in the stream for at least a month. What's worse, he demanded a four dollar fee to reset the bone! My mind raced—I had no way of paying four cents, let alone four dollars. But then, I remembered the shaving kit in my tent. Suddenly, I devised a solution.

No, I did not trade away the kit. Instead, I offered the doctor my services as a barber! After all, I told him, a gentleman such as himself ought to look like a gentleman. The doctor readily agreed. It was hard to do my best work, one-legged as I was, but I remembered every one of your lessons, Mr. Atwood. When I was through, the grizzled doctor looked more stylish than a Beacon Hill dandy!

Word of my talent has rippled through Stretch Neck Gulch and the nearby camps. I am almost embarrassed to mention the reward I collect for a shave—three dollars! And the miners are happy to pay it. I can barely keep enough shave liquid to meet the demand. My days as a gold miner are over. I've found a new sort of gold, I venture to say.

Here, however, is the best news of all. In these short weeks, I have earned enough to build a proper shop. The land is located in a nearby town called Auburn, right on the main road. By the time you receive this letter, my ankle will be healed and my shop in operation. So, if you wish to write back, I am pleased to say that you may finally do so. Direct any letters to Slade's Barber Shop on Mother Lode Highway, Auburn, California.

I hope that my news does you both proud. I have kept you both in my heart always. I would never have been able to persevere without my memories of you.

With love,

Rupert

Period Slang Glossary

reckon: guess
dearer: more expensive
verily: very much
see the elephant: to see it all, experience it all
lay: cost, price
no-account: disreputable, dishonorable
little end of the horn: left at a disadvantage; similar to "short end of the stick"
plum: entirely
pan: to sift through river water and rocks in search of gold
mighty: huge
express: mail service
candle-lighting: sundown, the time when candles are lit
right: real, true
drink: alcohol
smite: to hit violently
all possessed-like: in a rage, loudly and angrily
dumbstruck: shocked to silence
Beacon Hill: a wealthy area of Boston
dandy: a man of extravagant style

California Gold Rush

by Jill Fisher
illustrated by Dion Williams

It was the year 1848 when news spread about the discovery of gold in California. At that time, the average worker made approximately one dollar a day. A man working in a gold mine could earn up to thirty-five dollars a day. Some made even more! So, in the spring of 1849, what became known as the "Gold Rush" began. Thousands of people, mainly men, left their families and homes to head West in hopes of finding riches and a better life. They were known as "forty-niners" for the year in which they left. Most had never even left their hometown before.

Men traveled by land and by sea to strike it rich. They traveled from all parts of the world to gain in the wealth. The journey was extremely difficult because there was no quick and safe route. It would be one of the hardest experiences of their lives.

Many forty-niners traveled by covered wagon. They trekked across difficult land, crossed hot deserts, and climbed high mountains with their wagons, mules, and oxen. The trip took months, and the settlers were forced to face the wilderness and disease, camp outdoors, hunt for food, and cross dangerous rivers.

Others traveled by boat. But this journey was not a better experience than traveling by covered wagon. The trip was just as dangerous. They faced similar fears, such as accidents, lack of supplies, and disease.

Most people felt that their prayers were answered when they arrived in California. However, it was not as wonderful as they had dreamed. Gold was not as easy to find as they had imagined. In fact, most forty-niners did not find much gold or make a great deal of money.

As the quest for gold grew greater, the job became more dangerous. Men began fighting over gold and the claims to mines. Some forty-niners were violently attacked or even killed during this time period. As gold became more difficult to find, foreigners such as Mexicans and Chinese—and even the Native Americans—were driven out of the camps.

The Gold Rush lasted for about ten years. Once all of the gold that could be found by hand had been discovered, there was no more money to be made. The men did not have heavy equipment to extract the remaining gold from deep in the ground. After the rush ended, many mining camps turned into ghost towns.

However, by this time, California had a prospering economy due to farming and industry. Many men stayed and built a life in the great city of San Francisco. It was a booming town with a lot of fertile land to farm.

Also, many of the miners headed to Nevada in search of silver. Sadly, a great deal of men did not make it home due to accidents during the journey or while mining. Disease also killed a lot of miners.

The California Gold Rush not only changed the lives of many people, but made California the popular state it is today. While most did not discover great wealth, people all around the world knew the story of California and its land of riches.

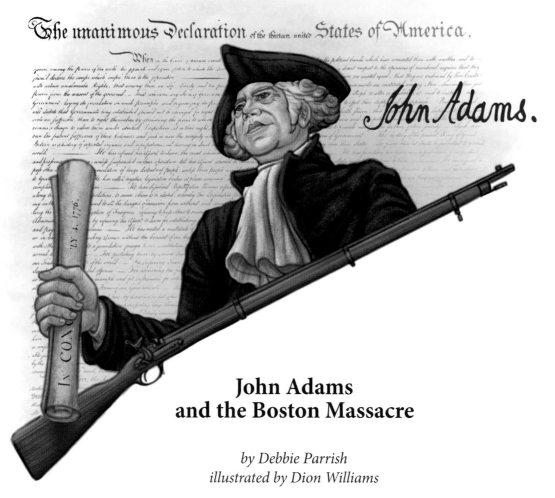

IN CONGRESS. JULY 4, 1776.

The unanimous Declaration of the thirteen united States of America.

John Adams.

John Adams
and the Boston Massacre

by Debbie Parrish
illustrated by Dion Williams

Everyone knows that John Adams was a dedicated patriot. He played a crucial role in the founding of our country. Everyone also knows that he was the second president of the United States. But not everyone knows that at one time, this dedicated patriot defended British soldiers against his fellow colonists in court. What would make this founding father seem to turn against his fellow patriots? What would make him insist on justice and fairness, no matter the consequences? To discover what made John Adams the respected man that he would become, we must start at the beginning of his life.

Early Years

John Adams was born in the year 1735 in Braintree, Massachusetts, about twenty miles south of Boston. His father was a hardworking farmer in this small town. In his early years, Adams learned the basics of reading and writing in a dame school. Dame schools met in private homes in one's community. After learning the basics, Adams continued his education in a Latin school. The Latin school was meant to prepare him for Harvard College, which sat just across the river from Boston. Adams's father had encouraged him to become a minister. After graduating from Harvard, though, the young man decided to teach.

Adams worked as a teacher just long enough to earn the money to study law. After two years of study, he began his legal career in Boston. Adams was so successful that after only a few years, he had more cases than almost any lawyer in the area.

Trouble in the Colonies

After a while, Adams felt that he was earning enough money to support a family. On October 25, 1764, John Adams married Abigail Smith, from nearby Quincy. He split time between his practice in Boston and his farm in Quincy. Adams's ideas on law, politics, and society became quite respected. He often wrote and published essays in the Boston newspapers. Adams shared with his readers many of his political ideas. He wrote about what he saw as growing troubles between Great Britain and the American colonists.

These growing troubles began with the French and Indian War. In this war, the British and the colonists fought the French and the Native Americans. The British had helped the colonies win the war, so the king demanded that the colonists help pay for the war. The king turned to Parliament, the part of the British government that makes laws. He asked it to pass laws to get money from the colonists. On the wishes of King George III, Parliament passed the Townshend Acts. The Townshend Acts forced the colonists to pay heavy taxes on paper, glass, and tea. These were goods that were imported, or brought over, to the colonies from England. When Parliament passed these acts, John Adams sided with his fellow colonists. He agreed with them that the taxes were extremely unfair. The colonists who lived in and around Boston refused to pay these taxes. Angered, the king sent soldiers to enforce the law.

Parliament passed another act as well. This one said that the colonists had to provide food and housing for the soldiers who were sent to make sure that they paid the required taxes. The colonists did not like having these British soldiers around. They resented the soldiers being in Boston. They resented even more that they had to feed and house them. They referred to them as "lobster backs" or "redcoats" because of the red uniforms they wore. Their tempers flared and their blood began to boil at the very sight of these "lobster backs."

John Adams believed it was wrong for the king and Parliament to demand these taxes. But he also disagreed with how some of his fellow colonists were protesting the taxes. As a lawyer, John Adams thought the protests should be done peacefully and through the legal system. Samuel Adams, John Adams's cousin, was also a lawyer. He showed his protest of the unfair taxes in a very different way from his cousin. Samuel Adams felt that violence and breaking the law made a much bigger statement. Sam was always doing some mischief to anger the British. Sam Adams and the men he ran around with were considered to be revolutionaries. This meant that they wanted complete independence from Great Britain. John Adams eventually became convinced that his cousin, Sam, was right. Nothing but complete separation would be acceptable.

John Adams became a strong spokesman for independence from the mother country, Great Britain. He was elected to the Massachusetts Assembly. Adams was chosen to be a delegate to the Continental Congress, and would go on to be one of the signers of the Declaration of Independence. Thomas Jefferson himself said, "I may have been the author of the Declaration, but Adams was the voice of independence." This was an important comment, because John Adams and Thomas Jefferson were not always very friendly with each other. When war broke out with England, it was John Adams who appointed George Washington to command the entire Continental Army during the Revolution.

So, if John Adams was such a patriot who spoke out for independence from England, how did it happen that he would end up defending British soldiers in court? What event forced Adams to make one of the most important decisions of his life?

The Boston Massacre

From the time that the first British soldiers arrived, the colonists made every effort to mock and hassle the "lobster backs." At times, the colonists even threatened the soldiers by telling them to beware of the concealed, or hidden, weapons they carried. Two British soldiers were even attacked and beaten. This made all the British regiments very concerned about what could happen to them.

The worst of these conflicts occurred on the night of March 5, 1770, in front of a building called the Customs House. The Customs House was where the taxes collected by the royal governor were kept. These taxes, called customs, were collected on imported goods and then sent to the king. The trouble started when a group of colonists began to mock and taunt a British soldier who was guarding the Customs House. When a group of soldiers led by British Captain Thomas Preston arrived to support the guard, the crowd turned on the entire regiment. Captain Preston ordered the colonists to leave and go home. The colonists refused. They stood their ground and dared the British soldiers to fire at them.

Captain Preston was in a very bad situation. He knew that it was against the law of the colonies for the soldiers to fire on civilians without orders from a court. He also saw that the colonists far outnumbered his soldiers. Not only did the colonists not leave and go home, but some of them began ringing the church bells. This was a call for many more colonists to join the group, which was already getting out of control.

The captain and his men lined up in columns. They crossed King Street with guns called muskets, which had bayonets fixed on them. The group of soldiers reached the lone British guard. The guard joined with the British marching columns. They intended to march back to the barracks, or sleeping quarters.

As the soldiers tried to leave, the colonists closed in and surrounded the regiment. They threw rocks, oyster shells, and hard packed snowballs at the soldiers. When one of the soldiers was hit by a stick, the soldiers opened fire. The colonists Crispus Attucks, Samuel Gray, James Caldwell, Samuel Maverick, and Patrick Carr were killed. Three of these colonists died immediately. Two others were wounded and died shortly afterward. Six other colonists were wounded. This historic incident became known as the Boston Massacre.

The word *massacre* is usually used when many people are killed. However, the colonists used the word for another reason as well. They wanted to stir up hatred for the redcoats. The silversmith, Paul Revere, even produced a picture from an engraving to send out to the other thirteen colonies. The people of Boston wanted the other twelve colonies to know what had happened so that they could gain support for independence.

There were many colonists who witnessed the tragedy. But these eyewitnesses did not agree on how it happened. One man claimed that he heard Captain Preston order his men to fire. But another witness said that the captain ordered the men not to fire. One colonist said that he saw someone throw a stick at one of the soldiers, and the soldier opened fire. Another witness claimed that he heard Captain Preston yell at his men for firing. With all of this conflicting information, how could one know who really was at fault?

The Royal Governor of Massachusetts, Governor Hutchinson, heard the news of the shooting and rushed to the scene. He questioned Captain Preston about what had happened. Hutchinson then climbed to a balcony overlooking the site and tried to calm the mob. He and his council ordered an investigation and made a decision. Captain Preston and eight of his soldiers were arrested, questioned, and sent to jail. The redcoats remained in jail for seven months until their trial. That's when John Adams entered the story.

The day after Captain Preston and the British soldiers were thrown in jail, Boston merchant James Forest went to thirty-four-year-old John Adams. At this time, Adams had a successful law practice in Boston. Forest asked him to defend the British soldiers. Adams knew that a decision to defend the British soldiers would be very unpopular with his fellow colonists. He knew it could cause him to lose many of his clients. Yet Adams had a deep faith and respect for the legal system and the rule of law. Though he wanted the British soldiers out of Boston, Adams believed that those accused deserved proper defense. John Adams was faced with the conflict of his life. Should he take the easy way out by not representing Preston, or do what he knew was right?

Everyone assumed that Adams would side with the colonists against the soldiers. He had argued case after case in court against the British. Just a few years before this event, Adams won an important case against the British Parliament concerning the right to a trial by jury. When Adams's friends heard that he was asked to defend the soldiers, they were shocked. They did not understand why he would even consider it.

Adams's patriot friends warned him not to take on such an unpopular case. They told him that the public would hate him. They said that any hopes he might have for a career in politics would be ruined. At this time, he was a representative of Boston in the general court. He had been appointed to this position by the colonists, and he knew that the colonists could remove him. Adams could be a very stubborn man, though, when it came to doing what he believed was right. No matter what might happen to him personally, Adams felt he owed it to his legal profession and to himself to do the right thing.

Before taking the case, however, Adams talked with his wife, Abigail. When he first told her that he had been asked to take the soldiers' case, Mrs. Adams burst into a flood of tears. She told her husband that she was quite aware of the danger her family could be put in. She worried about the safety of her husband and her children. This was a difficult time in their personal life. They had just lost their two-year-old daughter, Susanna. John Adams did not want to make life more difficult for Abigail than it already was. But Abigail understood her husband very well. She knew he would struggle with doing what was right, and she would support whatever decision he would make.

John Adams came to believe that his cousin and fellow patriot, Sam Adams, had planned the whole event to make the British soldiers look bad. Abigail agreed with her husband that the entire incident was a setup. John Adams knew that taking the case would make him very unpopular with his friends and neighbors, but he had to follow that voice within, his conscience. He wanted people to know that everyone has rights. He wanted everyone to know that even though they were the enemy, these soldiers would be treated fairly in the colonies.

Adams's Defense

Even before the trial took place seven months later, Adams sprang into action by writing a newspaper article of Captain Preston's side of the story. In the article, he tried to turn public opinion around. Adams wrote that it was the colonists who were the attackers and that the soldiers were only defending themselves. To make matters worse, Samuel Adams would be the lawyer who opposed him during the soldiers' trial. This was the same Sam Adams who was a troublemaker who stirred the colonists to revolution. John Adams wrote that he had come to approve of and even support independence for the colonies. But he still did not approve of the way Sam Adams was encouraging violence.

Captain Preston's trial began in late October of that year. The main question of the trial was whether Captain Preston gave his men the orders to fire. Three eyewitnesses swore that the captain did give the order, and four swore that he did not. A colonist named Daniel Calef was the witness who was most harmful to the captain's case. He said that the moon was shining brightly enough for him to see the captain. He swore that he was looking directly into his face when Captain Preston gave the order to fire.

When Captain Preston was questioned at the trial, he was asked if the colonists had asked whether or not the guns were loaded. The captain replied that he told them that they were loaded. But when asked if the soldiers intended to fire the guns, Captain Preston said he replied, "By no means." He said that immediately after that, one of the soldiers had been struck on the face by a stick. He told about how the colonists were using many heavy clubs to attack the soldiers. He said snowballs with rocks in them were being thrown at them. According to Captain Preston, it was at that point that three or four soldiers fired.

Adams looked at the jury which was made up of twelve colonists. He said that it just did not make sense that Captain Preston would give the order for the soldiers to shoot. After all, he was standing in front in the line of fire! Adams also claimed that the soldiers who did fire on their own did so in self-defense. He said they were trying to protect themselves from the colonists' attacks.

Witness James Bailey testified that he saw Crispus Attucks knock down one of the soldiers with a large stick of wood. Adams then turned to the jury and asked them if they would not have done the same thing to protect themselves. This was a wise question by Adams. He wanted the jury to imagine being in the same situation as the soldiers.

Adams's wisest decision as a lawyer was to put the doctor who had cared for the injured colonist, Patrick Carr, on the witness stand. The doctor shared Carr's last words. According to the doctor, Carr said that the soldiers took much abuse from the colonists before they fired. Just before dying, Carr also said that he forgave the soldier. He said that he had no hatred for the soldier because he was just trying to defend himself.

Adams also pointed out the ringing of the church bells. He said this was intended to bring more colonists to join the mob against the British soldiers. He said he believed that Sam Adams and his gang had planned the whole incident to make the soldiers look worse.

After every witness had given testimony, the judge told the jury that malice or hatred was the main point to remember about the case when making their decision. He said that to kill someone with hatred was murder. He pointed out that if it were not done with hatred, it would not be murder. Sam Adams said that Patrick Carr's words were "hearsay" since he was dead and not present to actually talk to the jury himself. Hearsay is not usually allowed in a trial, but in this case the judge allowed it. He said that since the words came from a dying man, he felt they could be trusted.

John Adams said these famous words to the jury: "Facts are stubborn things." He meant that it did not matter what someone thought of the event, or how he felt personally about the people involved. Those thoughts and feelings did not change the facts of the case. The jurors might not have liked the British soldiers, but that did not change what had really happened. Only the facts of the case were important. The judge then turned the case over to the jury to make a decision.

It took less than three hours for the jury to deliberate, or discuss and think about, the case. The jury found Captain Preston and six of the other soldiers on trial not guilty. That meant that these soldiers would go free. The other two soldiers, Hugh Montgomery and Mathew Killroy, were clearly proven to have fired at the colonists. They were found guilty of manslaughter. This meant that they did fire and kill someone, but they did not intend to kill. These two soldiers received a small punishment, but they did not have to serve any time in jail.

The Aftermath

When the colonists heard the jury's decision, they were very angry. Sam Adams was the loudest to disagree. He thought that the soldiers were guilty and had gotten away with murder. He wrote many letters about it to the newspaper. He criticized the verdicts, or decisions, the way the trial was conducted, and what he saw as a misuse of evidence. Even though the trial was over, the colonists would never forget the events of that night. John Adams recorded in his diary that he received many attacks in the newspaper and many public insults. Some rumors began that Adams had taken the case because he was offered a large sum of money. Adams answered that rumor when he stated that he had worked many hours and had many worries and sleepless nights, all for just eighteen guineas—about eighteen dollars.

The colonial leaders and his fellow patriots could not understand why Adams would take the side of the British. As expected, Adams lost a lot of business from his law practice in the next several months. When news reached Benjamin Franklin in Philadelphia, he had this to say about his friend: "Adams means well for his country, is always an honest man, often a wise one, but sometimes and in some things, is absolutely out of his senses."

But later, people began to understand. Adams was not taking the side of the British. He was taking the side of the law. After a few months, his law practice regained the business it had lost. History has judged him more kindly than his friends did. Rather than being criticized, Adams is now admired for such a courageous decision.

John Adams would go on to make many more important decisions during his lifetime. He helped to frame, or create, our country's Constitution. He served as a United States representative to France. Eventually, he was elected as the second president of the United States. John Adams made many other difficult decisions in his lifetime. Many of those decisions were not agreeable to all people, but Adams himself said that the decision to defend the British soldiers was the one of which he was most proud.

The History of "Yankee Doodle Dandy"

by Michael Scotto
illustrated by Kent Kerr

The folksong "Yankee Doodle Dandy" is the first national song of the United States. It is older than "My Country 'Tis of Thee," "God Bless America," and even "The Star-Spangled Banner." The catchy song was written during America's colonial days and has been a symbol of American pride since the nation was born. It is also the state song of Connecticut. However, when it was composed, the song was not intended to make Americans proud. In fact, "Yankee Doodle Dandy" was first written to insult and mock the American colonists.

Reading the lyrics of "Yankee Doodle Dandy" today, it might be hard to understand what was so insulting. To the modern eye, the song's first verse almost reads like nonsense.

Yankee Doodle went to town
A-riding on a pony
Stuck a feather in his cap
And called it macaroni.

To an American colonist, though, the connotations would have been very clear. Each line was meant to ridicule their culture. To understand the song's original meaning, one must learn a bit about the time in which it was written.

Not everyone agrees upon exactly when "Yankee Doodle Dandy" was written. Some historians argue that it was 1758. The Library of Congress dates the song to 1755. No matter the year, though, the song's composer was a British doctor named Dr. Richard Shuckburgh.

He wrote it during the French and Indian War. That was a war between Great Britain and France that took place in North America. At the time, America was not yet its own nation. It was still a cluster of colonies under British control. So, the American colonists, or colonials, joined forces with the British Army and helped them fight.

The British soldiers and the colonial militia were quite different in appearance. The Brits were clean-cut, always looking sharp in their red uniforms. The colonials, on the other hand, often did not even have uniforms. They simply marched in their threadbare work clothes. At the time, life in America was rough and rural. The colonials lived off of the land. Few had time for fancy dress, or even regular schooling.

Because of the colonials' seeming backwardness, the British soldiers looked down upon them. Dr. Shuckburgh wrote "Yankee Doodle Dandy" to express that feeling. But how does the song mock the colonials? A close reading can make it quite clear. The first two lines, "*Yankee Doodle went to town / A-riding on a pony*," contain several separate insults. The word *Yankee* was a putdown the British used to describe people from New England. The word *Doodle* meant "simple fellow"; a more current term could be "hick." In the second line, the speaker uses "A-riding" instead of "riding" to make fun of the colonials' lack of education and use of slang. Lastly, Yankee Doodle is riding a pony, which is meant to point out the colonials' poor resources. British soldiers rode majestic horses, while the colonials rode squat ponies, often straight off their farms.

The second two lines of the song are a bit harder to understand. After all, one might ask, how could anyone mix up a feather and macaroni? Even if the colonials were as backward and uneducated as the British thought, that seems a bit of a stretch. In the song, though, the word *macaroni* does not refer to pasta. In the 1750s, *macaroni* described a style of high European fashion. In Europe, clothing was growing more and more extravagant. Men's hats could be a foot tall, made entirely of fur. In these lines, "*Stuck a feather in his cap / And called it macaroni*," the writer is saying that

colonials are such simpletons that they think putting a feather in their shabby caps makes them stylish.

The refrain of the song continues the mockery. These four lines are repeated after each verse:

Yankee Doodle, keep it up
Yankee Doodle dandy
Mind the music and the step
But with the girls be handy!

The speaker encourages Yankee Doodle to keep it up—as if to say, "continue being such a fool; it makes me laugh." At the time of the song's writing, a *dandy* was any man of great style. Here, of course, it is used sarcastically. In the last pair of lines, the speaker tells Yankee Doodle to "mind," or "pay attention to," the music and the "step," or "type of dance." This is another mocking reference to colonial culture. The popular music and dance in the colonies was considered to be of lesser quality than British music and dance. The final line is yet another insult—this time aimed at colonial women. Basically, the speaker implies that colonial women are less honorable and moral than British ladies.

As one might guess, this song was very effective as a way of taunting colonials. It mocked their speech, clothing, education, music, and women. As time went on, it became popular among British soldiers to make up new mocking verses to the song. During the following twenty years, it is believed that over 190 verses were written to the song's tune. During this time, whenever they had the chance, British soldiers sang "Yankee Doodle Dandy" to taunt the colonials. They sang it as they passed through their towns. They even sang it outside their churches during Sunday services.

Eventually, though, the colonials became fed up with the abuse. As the Revolutionary War began, and the colonial army began to win some battles, the Americans turned the song around. The Americans would frequently sing "Yankee Doodle Dandy" after victories, adding their own verses. In this way, the mockers became the mocked. After one skirmish, the colonials made captured British soldiers dance to the song over and over, until they could not stand to hear it anymore.

That is how "Yankee Doodle Dandy," a song of mockery, became one of pride. The colonials were not well-educated, well-equipped, or stylish like the British. However, they were still capable of beating the British military—at the time, the greatest in the world. That is why even today, over 250 years after its writing, the song stands as a symbol of the American spirit.

The Importance of Protecting Endangered Species

by Nicole Costlow
illustrated by Brian Cibelli

The word *extinction* is a scary term. It means that a species of plant or animal has been eliminated from existence on the earth forever. Extinction is a very real threat to thousands of plant and animal species. Sadly, many species face extinction because of human actions. It is important not only to understand how our actions affect wildlife, but also to understand why humans should protect endangered species.

Awareness of endangered species began to grow in 1973 when government leaders passed the Endangered Species Act. This act is enforced by the US Fish and Wildlife Service. This act protects species that fall into two main categories: endangered and threatened. A species becomes *endangered* when it is very close to extinction. A *threatened* species is one that is not yet endangered, but is likely to become so soon. As of 2011, there were 1,383 endangered or threatened species of plants and animals in the United States alone.

Many animals are placed on the endangered or threatened list because humans are destroying their habitats, or where they live. In states like California and Utah, the habitat of the desert tortoise is shrinking due to the construction of new homes. Not only are desert tortoises losing their habitat, but many are killed by the heavy machinery used to build the new homes. Scientists estimate that only about one hundred thousand desert tortoises remain in the wild.

Another species that has suffered due to human interaction and development is the brown bear, commonly known as the grizzly bear. As the bears' natural, wooded habitat changes and disappears, they are forced into areas where humans live in order to find new food sources. When this happens, grizzlies are often shot and killed to keep humans safe. Also, during hunting season, hunters often mistake brown bears for black bears and kill them for sport. Today, brown bears are listed as a threatened species.

Global warming, or climate change, is another serious threat to endangered species. Scientists have found that our planet's temperature is rising. Most believe that this is due to gases released from the fuels many humans use in their daily lives. These gases get trapped in the earth's atmosphere and cause the planet's temperature to become warmer over time. The rising temperatures cause ice to melt in places like the Arctic. This process has caused creatures such as polar bears to be considered threatened animals under the Endangered Species Act.

Polar bears depend on the natural sea ice in the Arctic for their habitat and for hunting. Without it, they will have fewer places to find food and will have to swim farther distances to find a resting place. Scientists estimate that there are only about twenty-five thousand polar bears left in the wild. Two-thirds of that population may vanish within the next fifty years if Arctic temperatures continue to rise. That equals more than sixteen thousand polar bears that may be lost due to global warming.

The world's tiger population has suffered some of the greatest loss at the hands of humans. At one time, there were nine different types of tigers in the world. Over the past seventy years, three of those species have become extinct. Today, only a little more than three thousand tigers remain in the wild. The tiger population is shrinking for several reasons. Many were hunted for their fur; others lost their habitat as the human population expanded in countries such as India and China. Luckily for the tiger, organizations such as the World Wildlife Fund have begun efforts to save the species. Their goal is to double the world population of tigers by the year 2022.

There are many reasons why it is important for humans to help save endangered species from extinction. Our own survival may depend on it. Our planet is made up of many different ecosystems. Ecosystems are specific areas of living organisms that all depend on each other for survival. If one species in a particular ecosystem becomes extinct, all of the other living things in that ecosystem will be affected by the loss.

To understand how the extinction of a species can impact humans, it is important to think small. For example, in a forest ecosystem, a certain type of moss growing on a tree could provide shelter for hundreds of insects. Those insects leave their home in the moss to eat certain types of plants in the same forest. While feeding on those plants, the insects pollinate other plants in the forest that feed deer in the area. Humans who live near the forest use the deer as a food source. If the species of moss becomes extinct, the insects have no shelter and eventually die off. This harms the plants, which are no longer being pollinated and cannot grow. Without a plant supply, the deer are forced to move away to find another food source. Once the deer are gone, the humans in the area must find another source of meat for their meals. With the loss of just one species in an environment—even something as small as moss—the entire ecosystem could change forever.

In addition to saving endangered animal species, science has also proven that endangered plants could be extremely valuable to humans. Many medicines commonly used today contain substances from plants, including antibiotics and pain medications. In addition, medicines used to treat serious diseases, such as cancer, have come from plants. Today, there are 794 species of plants listed as endangered or threatened under the

Endangered Species Act. Even if only a few of these species become extinct, scientists will lose the chance to study them. They could miss out on finding cures and treatments for diseases that affect people all over the world.

It is very important to understand how our actions on the planet affect the natural world around us. Once extinct, a species, whether beautiful or valuable, is gone forever. When we allow a plant or animal to become extinct, we are not just hurting nature; we could be hurting ourselves.

Healthful Habits

by Jill Fisher
illustrated by CJ Kuehn

Do you think that it is important to have healthful habits? Some people do not. Many people in America and around the world live a life filled with video games, junk food, and lying on the couch. Watching television and playing video games, when done too often, can be very unhealthful. An inactive lifestyle can lead to unhappiness, poor health, and low self-esteem.

Experts say it is vital for people of every age to have a healthful, balanced lifestyle. They recommend that everyone find ways to be active, because good health can make people happier and feel better about themselves. The healthier a person is, the more productive he or she can become. When healthful habits are started at a young age, a person is more likely to grow into a healthy adult.

Have you ever rushed home to play your favorite video game or watch your favorite television program? Have you ever ignored your friends to stay indoors for television and games? If so, you may be spending too much time in front of the screen. Experts say that spending too much time watching television and playing video games can be unhealthful. It is recommended that young people spend no more than two hours per day playing video games or watching television programs. It is true that there are excellent video games and television shows that are both educational and entertaining. However, most children spend an average of four hours daily in front of the television alone.

Kids who spend too much time in front of the television or playing video games can be physically, socially, and emotionally behind their peers. They can often feel isolated and lonely because they miss out on interaction with their friends. It is very important that kids know how to socialize. A healthy child knows how to converse with friends and resolve conflicts through discussions. While technologies such as text messaging and email make life more convenient, it is important not to let them replace personal relationships. In addition, children shouldn't forget to talk to the important adults in their lives on a daily basis. They are the people who will help them learn to handle life's situations. It is important to maintain a special bond with them.

Children who watch too much television or play too many video games may not do as well in school because they are not spending enough time on their work. Also, it is important for a child to use his or her mind and be creative while playing. Activities like reading, playing outside, board games, puzzles, and art projects are more valuable, healthful ways of spending one's free time.

It is not wise to watch television shows or play video games that are violent or aggressive. This can lead to children who feel angry and want to fight. If a person sees violence often enough, it can convince him or her that violence is an appropriate way to solve problems. That can be a dangerous mistake. It's a good idea to play video games that are rated E for everyone. A child should always ask the grownups who care for him or her before playing a new game. He or she should also make sure that the adults approve of all television shows that are being watched, as well.

Has there ever been a time when your parent or guardian told you to go to bed, but you just couldn't pull yourself away from your television or game? You just had to see how the show was going to end, or you felt like you had to finish the game. Staying up late for television or games can be an unhealthful habit, because it can keep you from getting a good night's sleep. It can make you feel tired the next day. In fact, you may not do as well on your schoolwork because you cannot concentrate. It's a good idea to turn the technology off at least half an hour before bed and let your body unwind. It is important for people to have downtime and give their minds a break. Reading and quiet music can help your body relax.

Children who do not get enough sleep and spend too much time with television and video games are more likely to gain weight. They do not get enough exercise from physical activities such as riding bicycles, playing sports, and even doing chores. When you do not get enough exercise, you gain weight. Over time, this can lead to obesity and major health problems such as heart disease, cancer, breathing issues, and diabetes.

Many people like to eat snacks while enjoying their television and video games. If you like to enjoy a snack during these activities, try to make a healthful choice. For example, you could eat yogurt, fruit, vegetables, popcorn, or pretzels. It is best to put popcorn or pretzels in a bowl instead of eating out of the big bag. This way, you can measure how much you eat and avoid having too much. Try drinking water or milk. Avoid unhealthful snacks like soda, candy, and cookies. If you treat yourself to a sugary snack, remember to brush your teeth. That is another habit that will lead to good health. It is very important to brush your teeth two times a day and floss daily.

Now you have a better understanding of why it is so important to practice healthful habits. It is essential that people limit the time they spend watching television and playing video games. Yes, it may be difficult to turn the television and video games off at first. However, it is the responsible choice—the choice that will provide you with a more healthful life. A healthful life leads to a happy life.

The Life of Poetry

by Michael Scotto
illustrated by Dion Williams

What is poetry? That is a question poets and thinkers have tried to answer many times. The twentieth century American poet Paul Engle once wrote, "Poetry is boned with ideas, nerved and blooded with emotions, all held together by the delicate, tough skin of words." Engle's explanation of poetry is quite poetic in itself. Of course, poetry has no actual bones, nerves, blood, or skin. The description is a metaphor. A *metaphor* is a comparison that represents two separate things as being the same. Using metaphor, Engle compares poetry to a body. Like a body, a poem is a single object made up of several parts. Bodies have organs; poems contain words, feelings, and ideas. In both cases, these elements are layered, one atop the other. Engle's poetic language gives his writing several layers as well. However, it can be summarized in one key idea: that poetry is alive.

How can poetry be alive? Poetry can live through its audience. For example, British playwright and poet William Shakespeare died nearly four hundred years ago. Still, his love poems are often read aloud at wedding ceremonies, even today. The "skin of words" can be tough to understand, but an audience can still relate to the emotions and ideas beneath them. The meaning of the poetry lives on.

Also, like all living things, poetry changes over time. Poets invent new *genres*, or styles, of poetry to better share their ideas and feelings. As poets have created more and more ways of writing poems, the word *poetry* has come to mean many different things. It describes works ranging from the epic tales of the ancient Greeks to Chinese folk songs to nursery rhymes—even to the lyrics of rap music.

If poetry is alive, then in a way, the history of poetry is its life story. The story is older than books. Every culture has its own version. This essay will tell the story of poetry written in the English language. It will briefly visit the major periods of poetry and describe the poetic devices, or tools, which were most popular in them. Through these descriptions, the reader will learn about the ways that English poetry has lived over the centuries.

English poetry was born some time during the sixth century CE. To properly tell its story, though, one must start over a thousand years earlier, in ancient Greece. Ancient Greek poetry is one of the parents of English poetry. Certainly, it was a powerful influence. Most of the terms used to discuss poetry today come from the Greek language. For instance, the word *onomatopoeia* describes words that imitate sounds, such as *bark*, *sizzle*, or *crash*. Two of the most important terms in poetry, *rhythm* and *meter*, also come from Greek. The Greek word for rhythm, *rhythmos*, means "measured movement." Meter is one way of setting up a poem's rhythm. It shows the way that syllables should be accented when the poem is read. There are many kinds of meter. Each one describes a pattern that is repeated a specific number of times per line in a poem. Meter is not the only way of creating rhythm in a poem, but it has been one of the most popular.

In ancient Greece, rhythm and meter were not just important—they were necessary. This is because ancient Greek poetry was not written. It was performed aloud from memory. Poets traveled from town to town, sharing their work with different audiences. Greek poems can be read now, of course—but only the most popular ones. These poems were performed over and over until someone who could write copied them down. These poems are said to have "survived."

The most popular meter in ancient Greece was called *heroic hexameter*. The two most-celebrated Greek poems, the *Iliad* and the *Odyssey* by Homer, were both written in this meter. *Hex* is Greek for six, so each line of poetry always had six groups of syllables per line. This meter helped make poetry easier to remember and recite. The meter was called *heroic* because the most famous Greek poems were about Greek war heroes and their adventures. The stories were *epics*, or long poems about great events. To the Greeks, poetry was a way

to remember the things they held most dear. Poetry reminded the Greeks of their culture's greatness.

At first, Greek poets used only heroic hexameter. Over time, though, poets wished to share different kinds of stories. To do so, they created different meters, like *pentameter* (five groups of syllables per line), *tetrameter* (four groups), and *trimeter* (three). Each meter created a different rhythm. Each rhythm could give a poem a different tone, or feeling. Poetry also evolved as the Greeks created new genres besides the epic. Some styles are still used today. Others were lost when the Greeks were conquered and their civilization collapsed.

The first English poem did not appear until nearly one thousand years after the fall of the Greeks. It was not created in modern English. That did not yet exist. Rather, it was composed in Old English, which is an ancestor of the modern version. This first poem is called *Beowulf*. Like the *Iliad* and the *Odyssey*, it was a heroic epic. *Beowulf* was first put into writing around 1000 CE, but it had been performed by Anglo-Saxon poets up to three centuries earlier. As in ancient Greece, Old English poetry was first only performed aloud from memory.

To help their memories, Anglo-Saxon poets used different techniques from the Greeks. Instead of meter, Old English poetry used a method called alliteration. *Alliteration* is a technique where several words that begin with the same letter are used in a row. It is often used in nursery rhymes today, such as "Peter Piper," which states, "Peter Piper picked a peck of pickled peppers." Alliteration helped to create the rhythm of Anglo-Saxon poems. Since they used it so often, the Anglo-Saxon style of poetry is often called *alliterative verse*.

In 1066, the Normans of France conquered England. The era after the Norman invasion is called the medieval period. During the medieval period, the Normans brought many changes to English culture. The English language changed greatly. It grew closer to the modern English spoken today. This medieval language is known as Middle English. Of course, as the language changed, so did poetry.

Medieval poets wrote of different subjects than the Greeks and Anglo-Saxons. Where the older cultures' great poems were heroic epics, medieval poets wrote about religion and romance. As the topics changed, so did the styles. Medieval poets left alliterative verse behind. Instead, they relied on meter to build rhythm, like the Greeks. However, they also added something new: rhyme. Poets began to craft rhyming patterns for their work, such as the couplet. *Couplet* is the term for two lines of rhymed verse, such as:

In fourteen hundred ninety-two,

Columbus sailed the ocean blue.

The most well-known medieval poem, *The Canterbury Tales* by Geoffrey Chaucer, is written in couplets. Chaucer used the English language more richly than any poet had before. It would be almost two hundred years before another poet matched him.

The poet who finally topped Chaucer was William Shakespeare. Shakespeare wrote during a time known as the Renaissance. The Renaissance followed the medieval period. The word *renaissance* means "rebirth." It is a very fitting word when it comes to Shakespeare. Through his brilliant works, Shakespeare not only breathed new life into poetry and drama, he also helped to reshape the entire English language.

Shakespeare had a larger vocabulary than any poet before him. To write his plays and poems, he used nearly eighteen thousand different words. Of those eighteen thousand words, Shakespeare was the first to write at least two thousand of them. With his rich vocabulary and sensitive mind, Shakespeare perfected the popular forms of his day, like the sonnet. *Sonnets* are fourteen-line poems with a specific meter and rhyme scheme. Even though the form was very strict, Shakespeare's language made each of his 154 sonnets unique.

Shakespeare was not only a master of rhyming verse. In his plays, he used a form known as blank verse. *Blank verse* has a meter, but it does not rhyme. With blank verse, Shakespeare did not have to fit his ideas to a rhyme scheme. He was freer to communicate with his audience. Though he wrote no poems in blank verse, Shakespeare's plays greatly affected future poetry. *Paradise Lost*, the last great poem of the English Renaissance, was an epic written in blank verse.

After the Renaissance, several shorter poetic periods followed. In each period, poets had different thoughts on what poetry should express. They also felt very strongly about how poetry should be written. For example, after the Renaissance, many poets began to frown on Shakespeare's style. They believed that his writing was too rough around the edges, even sloppy. This belief helped to fire the next period in the life of poetry: the Augustan period.

The Augustan movement lasted from the late 1600s until about 1750. At that time, the British Empire was growing more and more powerful. The poets of this era wanted to match the greatness of their motherland. Poetry became more about wit and intelligence. It became not just a way of telling stories, but of making an argument. Augustan poets wrote in tidy, clever, rhyming couplets. They poked fun at society and each other. They even took classic poems like the *Iliad* and the *Odyssey* and "improved" them by rewriting them in their own style. Writing poetry grew into a sort of competition. Each poet wished to prove who was best educated, or funniest, or who could write the best couplet.

By the mid-eighteenth century, though, many began to tire of the Augustan style. Augustan poets had thought Shakespeare was too sloppy; the poets that followed thought the Augustans were too neat. To them, Augustans wrote without emotion—the nerves and blood of poetry. In a way, the new poets worried that the Augustans had sucked the life out of the art form. They were desperate to bring feeling back to it. For this reason, the next period became known as the Romantic period.

The Romantic poets wrote during a time of great change. It was a time of revolutions—the American Revolution, the French Revolution, and the Industrial Revolution. More and more people lived in cities. Machines were becoming a part of everyday life. The Romantics wrote poems that provided an escape. In the past, poets had written of many heroes and their adventures in battle. Romantics wrote about a new kind of hero: the poets themselves.

Romantics believed that the poet had a unique power. Anyone could fall in love, or become jealous, or enjoy a beautiful sunset. Only a poet, though, could find the right words and symbols to express those feelings. John Keats, one of the great Romantics, wrote that poetry "should strike the reader as a wording of his own highest thoughts, and appear almost a remembrance." He meant that when people read a poem, it should remind them of things they have felt before but never knew how to describe. Therefore, it was the poet's duty to live a rich life and write of his or her own experiences.

The time that followed the Romantic period is known as the Victorian era. This era lasted all the way until the early twentieth century. Victorian poets followed in the footsteps of the Romantics in many ways. Like the Romantics, Victorian poets were more interested in emotion and feeling than logic. They also wrote poems focused on their individual experiences. However, the Victorians used a wider range of techniques. They used many types of stanzas. A *stanza* is a grouping of several lines of poetry. They experimented with alliterative verse and unusual meters to create unique rhythms. They brought back old styles to express new ideas. By the turn of the twentieth century, poets could make a wider variety of poetry than ever before. Of course, there were limits. There were still certain rules that a "great poem" had to live by. Soon, though, a terrible event would change the life of poetry forever.

World War I lasted from 1914 to 1918. It was one of the bloodiest and most vicious wars in history. The war changed the way many looked at the world. People began to question how they lived their lives. They doubted the wisdom of their leaders. They lost interest in old traditions. Out of all this uncertainty, a new movement was born. It was called Modernism.

Modernists wished to reject everything that had come before. They despised tradition. They wished to break every rule, to shock the audience. The earliest Modernists were hard at work even before World War I. However, their work became much more accepted after the war. The world was finally ready for a drastic change.

In the Modernist era, poets did many experiments. For example, the famous Modernist poem *The Waste Land*, by T. S. Eliot, jumps between different moods, styles, times, and characters, all without warning. One of the biggest shifts, though, involved a form called *free verse*. Free verse does not use rhyme or meter. Its rhythm is created by its stanzas, word choice, and line breaks. The Modernists did not invent free verse, but they helped to make it mainstream. With their experiments, Modernists did not simply give poetry fresh life. They made it explode, and each fragment shot off in a different direction.

Modernism lasted through the middle of the twentieth century. After that period ended, many different poetic movements formed. They had names like the Beats and the Surrealists. There was even one group of poets in England called the Martians. Their idea was to write poetry about everyday things, but to write as if they were aliens seeing these things for the first time. Each movement, or school, of poets had a different way of viewing poetry. As a group, though, they can be described as Post-Modernists.

How does poetry live today? The Post-Modern era continues even now. One of the most recent popular styles is called *performance poetry*. Performance poems are not meant to be read on the page. They are recited from memory by the poet for a live audience. Performance poets often travel from city to city and share their work with small groups. This might sound familiar. While performance poetry feels new to young audiences, its roots are as old as poetry itself. After so many twists and turns, in a way, poetry has returned to its original home.

No one can guess what changes lie ahead. Nor can anyone guess what sort of poets will rise next. One thing is certain, though. Throughout history, poetry has been a way for people to connect. As long as poets find ways to connect with their audiences, whether the ways are old or new, poetry will continue to live on.

The Corps of Discovery Explores the Core of America

by Debbie Parrish
illustrated by Sean Kennedy

Today, the United States is a vast country that stretches from the Atlantic to the Pacific Ocean. It was not always so large, though. When our country was very young, it consisted of just thirteen states along the East Coast. In 1803, the United States purchased a huge tract of land from France. The deal was known as the Louisiana Purchase. For fifteen million dollars, the United States doubled in size. This land was west of the Mississippi River and stretched all the way to what is now North Dakota. The US Congress and Thomas Jefferson, the third president, knew that it was a wise purchase. They did not know, however, exactly what they had bought. The land had not been fully explored or mapped.

President Jefferson asked Congress to approve money for an exploratory expedition. He had two objectives for his request. The first was to gain information on natural resources and the Native Americans in the Northwest. The second was to find something called a Northwest Passage. From the time that the first European explorers had come to North America, men had sought a northern water route from the Atlantic to the Pacific Ocean. The United States thought that maybe, with the Louisiana Purchase, a northern waterway could be found to carry on trade with Asia.

To complete the expedition, Jefferson chose his secretary, Captain Meriwether Lewis, and William Clark, who were both experienced Army officers. Lewis and Clark selected thirty-one other men to join them.

This group would be named the Corps of Discovery. Before setting out on their long journey, the explorers had much preparation to do. To help with navigation, Lewis and Clark studied astronomy. They also learned botany, medicine, and biology. In addition, they made a list of supplies they would need to take with them. The list included guns, ammunition, medical supplies, scientific instruments, books, and food.

The expedition began near what is now St. Louis, Missouri, in May of 1804. The Corps followed the Missouri River through Kansas and Nebraska. Not all of the men in the Corps of Discovery made it the entire journey. One died just two months into the trip, and three were dismissed because they were causing trouble. To replace these men, Lewis and Clark recruited two fur traders. Sacagawea (pronounced *sah-KAH-guh-WEE-uh*), the Shoshone wife of one of the fur traders, became one of the expedition's most valuable members.

The Corps traveled in two small boats and a big keelboat. In the deep waters of the Missouri, they could travel freely. When the water became too shallow or rocky, they had to portage, or carry the boats over land. In August, the Corps of Discovery met a group of Native Americans in present-day Omaha, Nebraska. They handed out peace medals that were gifts sent by President Jefferson. Lewis and Clark gave speeches saying that the Native Americans now had a new "great father" to the east who promised peace and prosperity if the tribes did not make war with new settlers. Farther along the river in what is now South Dakota, the men witnessed the birth of a Native American baby. Lewis and Clark wrapped the baby in an American flag and proclaimed him to be an American.

When the Corps reached the Great Plains, they saw animals they had never seen before: antelopes, coyotes, and mule deer. By the end of the journey, the men had listed 178 plants and 122 animals never before recorded in science. Lewis and Clark preserved as many specimens as they could to take back to President Jefferson.

In present-day Bismark, North Dakota, the men found a village of almost five thousand Native American earth-lodge dwellers. Sacagawea was extremely helpful in trading and negotiating with these Native Americans. In winter, Clark noted that the temperature was forty-five degrees below zero, "colder than I ever knew it to be in the States." Since it was too cold to travel, the Corps of Discovery built Fort Mandan and settled in for the winter.

In January 1805, the Mandan tribe had a ceremony called the "buffalo calling." When a herd of buffalo came, the Native Americans and the explorers hunted together. Also, during that winter, Sacagawea gave birth to a baby boy. A Native American helped Lewis deliver the baby by giving Sacagawea a medicine made from crushing the rings of a rattlesnake.

When spring came, Lewis and Clark sent twelve men back down the Missouri River in the big keelboat loaded with specimens for Jefferson. These included Indian corn, skins of previously unknown animals, mineral samples, and five live animals. The weather was now warm enough for the Corps of Discovery to continue their journey west on the river.

Upon reaching Montana, Lewis and Clark were amazed at the wildlife, especially the large herds of buffalo. Lewis and one of his men encountered a grizzly bear near the Yellowstone River. They had heard stories of how large and ferocious the grizzlies were from the Native Americans, but they didn't believe these stories until they saw one first hand. In the days to come, the Corps saw more and more grizzlies.

Lewis and Clark were careful to map the previously unrecorded plains. They named rivers and landmarks after crew members. In honor of her skill at negotiating with Native tribes, they named a river after Sacagawea. When Clark saw a particularly beautiful river, he named it Judith after a girl back in Virginia whom he hoped to marry.

By the end of May, the Corps of Discovery arrived at the White Cliffs of the Missouri River. These remarkable cliffs are sandstone formations. After passing the White Cliffs, the explorers came to a fork in the river. They had to decide whether the true Missouri was the northern branch or the southern branch. Most of the men thought they should travel the southern route, but

Lewis and Clark thought otherwise. The captains had been told by Native Americans that the true Missouri contained a huge waterfall. The men agreed to follow their captains, and sure enough, within a few days, they came to the Great Falls of the Missouri. According to Lewis, it was the "grandest sight" he had ever seen.

After the Great Falls, the Corps saw so many more falls that they had to carry their boats by land. They buried most of their supplies and collections and built carts in order to carry the boats over steep, rocky terrain. The sun beat down on them and hailstorms pelted them. Travel became so rough that what should have taken only a half day by water took almost a month.

By late July, the explorers had reached the Three Forks of the Missouri. Lewis and Clark named the three branches: the Jefferson, after the president; the Madison, after the secretary of state; and the Gallatin, after the secretary of the treasury. These three men were responsible for the idea and for urging Congress to give money for the trip. As the Corps headed southwest on the Jefferson branch, Sacagawea began recognizing landmarks that she had seen before. She had at one time lived in this area before she was captured and taken back east.

The Jefferson River was shallow, which made it hard for the men to drag their boats upstream. Sacagawea recognized Beaverhead Rock, near present-day Dillon, Montana. She told the captains that they were nearing the headwaters of the Missouri River. By the middle of August, the explorers ascended the final ridge towards the Great Continental Divide of the Rocky Mountains. This peak, on the present-day border of Montana and Idaho, is where the rivers flow west and empty into the Pacific Ocean. What an exciting find for the Corps, since one of the main objectives of the expedition was to find a northern water route to the Pacific Ocean! They felt they were nearing the end of their journey. Looking over the peak, though, they found only more mountains instead of water. Their excitement changed to disappointment.

To cross these mountains, Lewis and Clark knew they would need horses. A nearby Shoshone tribe proved to be good luck for the Corps. Sacagawea began translating and found out that the Shoshone chief was her brother! They named the place Camp Fortunate. The Shoshone chief loaned the Corps twenty-nine horses, a mule, and a guide who led them through a mountain pass to present-day Missoula, Montana. He told them that when the corps passed the Great Falls, they missed a shortcut that would have saved them about fifty days of travel.

As the Corps of Discovery ascended the Bitterroot Mountains, the Shoshone guide lost the trail because it became so steep and rocky. When the men looked ahead, all they could see was range upon range of more mountains. They ran out of food and almost starved before they could get to modern-day Idaho, home of the Nez Perce. Lewis and Clark made friends with these Native Americans, who gave them all the food they could eat. They also showed the crew how to use fire to hollow out trees for canoes.

The men traveled down the Snake River where it joined the Columbia River. The Corps found that the Columbia was full of salmon. They caught and dried it in the sun to take with them. They could see Mount Hood in the distance. This sighting proved that they were on track with their map and near the Pacific Ocean, but first they had to descend the raging falls of the Columbia to arrive in the semi-deserts of Washington and Oregon. After traveling across these semi-deserts, Clark recorded in his journal entry for November 7, 1805, that he could see "an ocean in view."

In late November, the men had to decide where they would spend the winter. They voted to cross the Columbia and build their winter camp at modern-day Astoria, Oregon. During the winter, the men became terribly homesick and suffered through terrible rains. In fact, there were only twelve days without rain.

In March, Lewis and Clark presented their winter camp to the Native Americans, the Clatsops, and finally set out for home. On their return trip, the Corps split into four groups. With help from Sacagawea, Clark's group arrived in the Great Plains. Clark wanted to honor Sacagawea, so he named a huge sandstone landmark near Billings, Montana, "Pompy's Tower" after her son. On the sandstone tower, Clark carved his name and the date.

Lewis and his men camped overnight with a Blackfoot group, and during the night, the Blackfoot tried to steal the men's horses. In the fight that followed, the Corps killed two Blackfoot warriors. This was the only bloodshed during the entire journey. Lewis and his group met up with the other three groups at the mouth of the Yellowstone River. When the Corps arrived at the Mandan villages, they said goodbye to Sacagawea, her husband, and their little son.

As they headed home on the Missouri, they began to meet many boats of settlers who were headed west.

On September 23, 1806, the Corps reached St. Louis. They had been gone nearly two and a half years and had traveled over four thousand miles. By the time Lewis and Clark returned to Washington, they were considered national heroes. Lewis was made governor of the Louisiana Territory. Clark was made Indian agent for the West.

The Corps of Discovery did not find a practical northern waterway, but they did find and map many regions that became useful for future explorers and settlers. Upon returning, Clark did marry his dear Judith, and they named their oldest son Meriwether Lewis Clark.

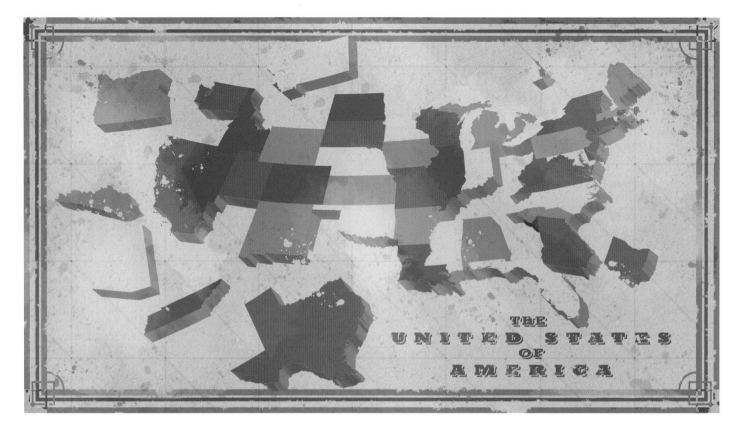

How the United States Was Shaped

by Jill Fisher
illustrated by Josh Perry

In 1776, the year of its founding, the United States of America consisted of only thirteen colonies. Today, however, America is composed of fifty states. Forty-eight of these states are located between two countries and three large bodies of waters. These states are known as the continental, or mainland, United States. The nation of Canada borders the mainland to the north, while Mexico meets its southern border. The bordering bodies of water are the Pacific Ocean on the west, the Atlantic Ocean on the east, and the Gulf of Mexico along parts of the south. The remaining two states are separate from the mainland. The forty-ninth state, Alaska, is divided from the mainland by Canada. Alaska is located about five hundred miles northwest of the state of Washington. The fiftieth state, Hawaii, is even farther away. Made up of a group of islands in the Pacific Ocean, Hawaii is over two thousand miles southwest of California.

Each of the fifty states has a unique shape and size. Many factors affected the crazy borders of the jigsaw puzzle that make up the United States. Some borders were created by natural elements, such as rivers, lakes, volcanoes, and mountain ranges. However, military battles, historical events, railroads, the government, and more played a hand as well.

Mother Nature helped to create some of the more oddly-shaped states with her enormous mountain ranges, dangerous volcanoes, great lakes, and powerful rivers. Twelve states have borders that are marked by active or potentially active volcanoes. They are Alaska, Arizona, California, Colorado, Hawaii, Idaho, New Mexico, Nevada, Oregon, Utah, Washington, and Wyoming. Many other states are divided by rivers. For example, the southern part of Ohio is lined by the Ohio River. This river marks the border between Ohio and the states of West Virginia and Kentucky.

Over time, some rivers have shifted due to erosion. That makes some parts of states appear to be on the wrong side of the rivers that originally marked their borders. For example, part of Indiana's border was originally marked by the Wabash River. Today, though, there are small parts of Indiana that are on the wrong side of this river. They look like they are part of Illinois due to the Wabash River gradually shifting over a long period of time. Obviously, this can be quite confusing.

Another reason for confusing borders between the states is human error. Long ago, when the states were created, men surveyed the land using transit and compass, chronometer, and astronomical readings. They also relied on information from previous surveys. They did the best they could with the given tools and situation. The border between the states of Georgia and Tennessee is still debated today. People say the original border is incorrect and needs to be changed. It is believed that the surveyor started at the wrong location. In fact, there are some homes that use Georgia addresses, even though they are technically in the state of Tennessee.

State boundaries have also been formed by historical events, such as the Louisiana Purchase, the creation of the Mason-Dixon Line, and the Oregon Treaty. The Mason-Dixon Line, for instance, takes its name from two surveyors named Charles Mason and Jeremiah Dixon. They helped to settle a dispute in colonial times over where Pennsylvania ended and where the colonies to the south of it began. The line these men mapped forms the southern border of Pennsylvania and the western border of Delaware. It sets these states off from Maryland and West Virginia (which was still part of Virginia when the line was drawn).

Look carefully at a map of America. You will notice how the states on the eastern side of the country have crooked borders and widely varying sizes. The states farther west look more like organized squares with straight lines. That is because people occupied the eastern side early in the country's history, with each state making its own rules. However, as the United States expanded westward, the American government made laws about how to form the states. In fact, most borders beyond the original thirteen colonies were created by Congress, which gave the states a more uniform shape and size. Often, they used the lines of longitude and latitude to determine the size and shape of each state.

Some states are very large while others are tiny. As the states were being formed, many people believed that all states should be the same size. In fact, back in 1786, Thomas Jefferson predicted the large territory of California would crumble into smaller states. Despite border battles, the gold rush, and even earthquakes, that did not happen. Another large state, Texas, was created with the intention of dividing it into five smaller states. Obviously, that did not happen either.

It is clear that many forces have affected the size and shape of each of the states. Over time, Mother Nature will continue to change the earth, and there may be more historical events that change the shapes of the states. Will the map of the United States ever look different than it does now? Only time will tell.

Saturn

by Summer Swauger
illustrated by Kevin Dinello

Saturn is one of the most recognizable and mysterious objects in the sky. It is the sixth planet from the sun, and the second largest in the solar system. The planet is named for the Roman god Saturn, who is known as Cronus in Greek mythology. Saturn is the farthest planet that can be seen from Earth without the aid of a telescope. Ancient people on Earth observed Saturn and tracked its progress across the sky. In 1610, the astronomer Galileo became the first to see Saturn through a telescope. Since then, scientists have learned many things about this far-off planet.

Saturn and Earth are very different. Saturn is much larger than Earth. At its widest part, Saturn is about 120,500 kilometers wide. That is 9.5 times the diameter of Earth. Saturn's mass is 95 times greater than the mass of Earth. In fact, Saturn could hold 764 planet Earths inside of it.

Although Saturn is much larger than Earth, it is less dense. Saturn is one of the gas giant planets. These are sometimes called the Jovian planets, meaning "Jupiter-like." Saturn, like Jupiter, Uranus, and Neptune, is called a gas giant because it is mostly made up of gases. Scientists believe that Saturn is made up of about 96% hydrogen. It also contains small amounts of helium and other elements. Because of this, Saturn is the least dense planet in the solar system. It has only one-eighth the density of Earth. Saturn is even less dense than water, which means that it would float.

Only a small portion of Saturn is solid material. Scientists think that Saturn has a small, rocky core. It is extremely hot inside the core, measuring almost 12,000 degrees Celsius. Because it is so hot, most of the core cannot stay in a solid form. Therefore, the core is surrounded by a vast ocean of liquid elements. Above the liquid, the atmosphere turns into clouds of gases.

This atmosphere contains some of the fastest winds in the solar system. Winds in the upper atmosphere can reach 500 miles per second. In contrast, the fastest winds detected in Earth's atmosphere only measure 110 miles per second.

Saturn, like the other planets in the solar system, rotates and revolves. It takes the planet about 10.5 hours to complete one rotation. So, one full day on Saturn is less than half of one Earth day. But because Saturn is so far from the sun, it takes the planet about 30 Earth years to complete one revolution around the sun. On Saturn, there are 24,232 days in one year. Due to the planet's slow revolution, it has only revolved around the sun 13 times since Galileo first observed it more than 400 years ago.

Saturn's most unique and most well-known feature is the band of rings that encircles it. The rings look solid, but they are actually made of ice particles, dust, and rock. Saturn's moons, called shepherd moons, give the rings their shape. The moons' gravitational forces hold the rings in place. The exact number of Saturn's rings is not known, but scientists have identified seven main ring groups. They are called A, B, C, D, E, F, and G. Each ring group is made up of many smaller rings and divisions between the rings. The entire system of rings measures about 280,000 kilometers across. However, the rings are only about one kilometer thick, which is why they appear flat when viewed through a telescope.

Saturn has many moons orbiting it. So far, scientists have identified 62 moons of varying sizes, although there may be more that have not been discovered yet. Titan is Saturn's largest moon. It is the second largest moon in the solar system. In fact, Titan is bigger than Mercury, the planet closest to the sun. Rhea is Saturn's next largest moon. It is the ninth largest moon in the solar system. But Enceladus, which is Saturn's sixth largest moon, may be the most interesting. In 2008, scientists discovered the possible existence of water below the moon's surface. If this moon has water, it might also be able to support life. Even though Enceladus is only about as wide as the state of Arizona, it may be the most livable place beyond Earth in the entire solar system.

In July 2004, the Cassini-Huygens space probe became the first spacecraft to enter Saturn's orbit. It is the fourth spacecraft to visit the Saturn system. The spacecraft is made up of the Cassini orbiter and the Huygens space probe, which separated on December 25, 2004. Cassini completed several orbits of the planet, studying the rings and discovering new moons. On January 14, 2005, the Huygens probe landed on Titan. This was the first landing in the outer solar system, and it remains the farthest landing of any spacecraft launched from Earth.

The Cassini-Huygens mission was so successful that it received two extensions. It is now known as the Cassini Solstice Mission. Cassini will continue to orbit Saturn and some of its moons until 2017, when it is scheduled to enter Saturn's atmosphere to study the summer solstice in the planet's Northern Hemisphere. It will conduct the first study of a complete Saturn season. There is still much to learn about this distant planet, but new technologies are making it easier for scientists to solve the mysteries of Saturn.

The World at Your Fingertips

by Debbie Parrish
illustrated by Doyle Daigle

What is electronic, connects people from all over the world, and has been around much longer than you might think? It is used in our everyday lives. Do you give up? It's the Internet! Most people think of the Internet as a very recent technology. But the first version of the Internet was developed over forty years ago. It was called ARPAnet. It was a special network made in 1969 for the United States military. The military needed this network so that its computers could share information even if they were whole states apart. By the 1980s, similar networks were developed for civilians. These networks linked together and grew into the Internet that we use today.

Today's Internet can connect every computer using it, all around the world, like a giant web. Because of this, the Internet is often known as the World Wide Web. We refer to being connected on the Internet as being "online." The Internet is a great source of information and a way to communicate with others. It is also a huge source of entertainment. Can you imagine your life without this modern marvel? Just what is the Internet and what is it used for?

Internet Use

With so many computers linked together, there must be a huge amount of information on the World Wide Web. How do you find what you are looking for? Imagine all of the information inside all of the books in a huge library. How do you find the right shelf, book, and page? The library is organized to help you locate information, and so is the Internet. Just like every book in a library has its own call number, every page on the Internet has its own address. Sometimes you might not know the specific address for the information you want. If you don't, you can use a search engine to help you. When you type a keyword into a search engine, it searches the Internet for pages on which that word appears. Often, a search engine will suggest many sources of information from which you can choose.

Search engines are very helpful for people who need to find information. A search may be done just to satisfy your curiosity, or it may be used to find information for a school report. Imagine you and a friend are arguing over who had the highest batting average last year. Rather than arguing, you could quickly find this information using the Internet. Now suppose you have to write a report on Benjamin Franklin. You already know some things about Franklin's life, but you need more information. You need dates, place names, and specific accomplishments. The Internet is a great way to find all of the information you need and more.

Select one of the many search engines available and enter the keywords *Benjamin Franklin*. Hundreds of websites will come up, giving you suggestions on places to search. Each suggestion will include a brief description of the site. There is no end to the information available to you. The site you select will give additional links to more specific information. You will probably learn more than you first expected to. Sometimes your search for information on one subject will create interest in something entirely new.

When you are doing research, make sure you always use sites that give accurate information. Some sites allow anyone to write anything without checking the facts. A good rule is to find out who put the information on the Internet. If an author's name is listed, you can research that person to see if he or she is trustworthy. You should also look for the date on which the material was published. You want your information to be current. A reliable site will also stick to the main idea. If the information uses opinions rather than facts, it is probably biased for or against your subject. A site like this should not be trusted. If you find many spelling errors, chances are the material is not trustworthy. Always use accurate information and list where it came from.

Aside from search engines, the Internet has many other tools that can help with learning. For example, imagine that you are reading a book that has unfamiliar vocabulary words. If this happens, you can find an online dictionary, type in the word you want to learn, and get instant help. Many readers keep a dictionary website on hand the entire time they are reading challenging material. Other websites offer quizzes on books you may be reading. Many of these sites are arranged like games and contests.

In addition to learning, there are many other aspects of life that can be made easier with the Internet. Someone can order pizza, find and order a new pair of soccer cleats, or reserve tickets for the movie theater. People can find magazines, books, and music for sale. This can only be done with the permission and help of a parent or another responsible adult. You may do the search and browsing to find what you are looking for, but the adult must take care of the order and payment.

The Internet is also incredibly helpful when it comes to communication. You might have a friend, relative, or pen pal living far away. Rather than calling or writing a letter, you can email. That is, you can type a letter on your computer and send it electronically. Just like regular mail, you must have the person's address. But unlike regular mail, email is much faster. For example, if a friend were to visit Australia, thanks to email you would be able to keep up with where he was and what he was seeing during his entire trip. Not only could he send messages about his trip, he could also send pictures. You would almost feel as if you were there with him!

Another form of online communication is the chat room. This is a way for young people to talk with other young people. You must be very careful when using a chat room. Be sure that a parent helps you locate a safe one. Safe chat rooms are monitored electronically or by someone who previews what is written before it can be read online. In well-monitored chat rooms, you can meet people from around the world who share your interests while in a safe environment. You can talk with teachers, community leaders, scientists, and writers you may not ordinarily meet. You can learn a lot from other people's ideas.

A third kind of online communication is video chat. This is done using a webcam, which is a special camera that can be used to send live video between two computers. It is a great way to talk with people "face-to-face" even if they live all the way across the world. However, it is best to only use this form of communication with adult permission, and only with people you already know in real life.

For those who want to stay in touch with a large number of people at once, the Internet has many social websites. These websites provide a means of communicating with many friends or relatives at the same time. You must be very careful, however. Remember that the Internet connects your computer with everyone else who has a computer. You must be careful about what you share online and how you share it. There are controlled ways to keep you safe. Always check with your parents when you use these safe sites for young people.

If you are not searching for information or talking with friends, then you are probably using the Internet for entertainment. There are many online games for young people. Some are just for fun, and others teach while you are having fun. Just tell a search engine to look for *games for young people*, and it will suggest more sites than you can imagine. Some games allow you to compete with other players from all around the world. This sort of connection was impossible before the Internet.

You can also watch movies and many of your favorite television programs online. You can also watch sports contests live. Another huge source of entertainment is music. There are music sites that have every kind of music ever recorded. All of the entertainment you can imagine is available on the Internet, but you must get permission from your parent or guardian. He or she will know what is appropriate and safe for you.

Safety

Safe use of the Internet is important. The Internet can be a wonderful source of information, but its use can also pose hazards. Just like any tool, the Internet is safe if you follow a few rules. The most important rule

for young people is to always get permission and help from a responsible adult when using the Internet.

Sometimes you may find material online accidentally that makes you feel uncomfortable. You may enter a subject in a search engine and be directed to something entirely inappropriate. Always tell your parent or guardian if you happen on something that you feel is not appropriate. There are many helpful and fun websites that you can use safely.

The Children's Online Privacy Act is a federal law that protects young people using the Internet. It is designed to keep anyone from obtaining a child's personal information without a parent's permission. Even with this law, it is still important to talk with your parent or guardian and get permission before you do anything online.

One way that inappropriate or harmful information finds its way to you is through pop-ups. This could happen when you are reading an article or playing a game. All of a sudden a smaller screen pops up from out of nowhere. When this happens, do not click on and open the site. Close it immediately. If the pop-ups continue to appear, close the site you are using and tell an adult. Pop-ups can often expose your computer to viruses. Viruses are harmful programs that attack computers. Viruses can destroy your information or completely ruin your computer. There is probably a virus protection on your computer. Even so, you should be careful not to invite a bad program by opening a pop-up or link that you are not sure of.

There are many other important tips to remember in order to stay safe online. Never give out personal information such as your name, address, or phone number. Never send a picture to anyone without asking your parent or guardian first. Remember that you cannot really see or know for sure if people online are who they say they are. Not everyone is honest. Any adult who wants to cause harm can put a child's picture online and say he is nine years old. Talking online to people you do not know is the same as talking to strangers.

Above all, never meet someone in person who has tried to contact you on the Internet. Some people may claim to be your age and have the same interests as you. They may even put pictures online to make you think they are quite harmless. Always tell a responsible adult when someone suggests meeting in real life.

Netiquette

The Internet, just like the world in which you live, has rules that people should follow. Growing up, you have likely been taught manners such as saying "please" and "thank you." There is also a set of manners for the Internet. One nickname for this set of manners is "netiquette." *Netiquette* is formed from the words *net* and *etiquette*. Netiquette is a set of rules for behaving properly online. These rules cover the information you give out, the information you take in, and how to deal with people you communicate with on the Internet.

There is one main rule to follow when using the Internet: avoid hurting others' feelings. Remember that when you are communicating online, people cannot hear your tone of voice or see your facial expressions. You may say something jokingly, but the other person may take it seriously. This can lead to hurt feelings. You may have to make sure the person you're sending it to will know whether you are happy, sad, angry, or joking. You can do this by using words, or by using symbols such as :-) and :-(.

In turn, if someone sends you an email or a message that you take as insulting, stop and think that he or she may not have intended to hurt your feelings. You were not really there personally, so you may be taking it the wrong way. Give others the benefit of the doubt. Stay calm. Email that person back and question his or her intentions. More importantly, get a grown-up's advice about the matter. Don't start an argument, or "flame war," where you immediately send an insulting message back. This can get quite ugly and lead to broken friendships.

Another rule to keep in mind is to always respect other people's online rights. If someone were to make prank phone calls or send threatening letters to your house, it would be annoying or even scary. The same is true online. If someone sends you an email or threatening message, be sure to tell a parent or an adult right away. Never answer the threat with an email. Let an adult handle this.

Just as it is wrong to bully people face-to-face, it is wrong to bully someone on the Internet. Always think about what may hurt your feelings; that kind of behavior can certainly hurt someone else. If someone tries to get you to join in on bullying another person, or if you are being bullied on the Internet, do not respond. Don't get caught up in bullying online. Stay strong. This behavior is not only bad netiquette, it is against the law. Anything you write on the Internet can be retrieved by authorities. Remember to do the right thing.

Also, be polite with regard to discussion groups. People on the Internet sometimes get together online to talk about things they may have in common, such as last night's baseball game or the birthday party planned for tomorrow. If you want to join in the discussion, you should ask permission first. Do not crash a group just for the fun of ruining the discussion. People will definitely not think that is funny.

Just like with a face-to-face talk with a friend, be sure to keep private conversations private. If someone tells you something that is not to be shared, keep it to yourself. This also includes passwords, full names, addresses, and phone numbers. In fact, sharing passwords or very personal things about yourself is never a good idea, even with a close friend. Your personal information and others' personal information should be kept private.

Good netiquette leads to being responsible. Never use the computer to hurt other people. Taking things which do not belong to you such as files, pictures, or passwords is not being responsible. If you are using a shared computer, whether at home or in a public library, be polite. Do not take up all of the time. Be sure to close the programs you are using and leave the computer and area as you found them.

The Internet is a technology that has changed the world. With proper, safe, and polite use, it can enrich your life and the lives of those close to you. Happy browsing!

The Bard of Scotland

by Michael Scotto
illustrated by Matthew Casper

The Ploughman Poet, Rob Mossgiel, the Bard of Ayrshire, or simply Rabbie—Robert Burns was a man of many names. Though he died over two hundred years ago, he remains one of the world's most beloved poets. To the people of Scotland, he is their national bard. In America, there are more statues dedicated to Burns than to any native poet. On New Year's Eve, millions around the world celebrate by singing his most famous song, "Auld Lang Syne." This poem is about remembering good times gone by.

In "Auld Lang Syne," the speaker urges the audience to recall positive memories and to remember the acquaintances, or friends, who were part of them. The poem is about honoring one's influences, or showing respect for the people and events that have changed one's life. In his short life, Robert Burns had many influences. Each contributed in different ways. Some gave him love; some gave him education; and, of course, many of them, whether they knew it or not, inspired him to write. In a way, the story of Burns's life is also their story.

Robert Burns was born on January 25, 1759, in an area of Scotland called Ayrshire. His family worked as tenant farmers. Tenant farmers could not afford to buy land. Instead, they were forced to rent farms from wealthy landlords. It was a very hard way to make a living and Robert's family often suffered in poverty. Even so, Robert's parents tried to educate him as best they could.

Robert's mother, Agnes, could barely read or write. However, she knew many old Scottish folksongs. She sang them all to Robert during his boyhood. When Robert grew older, he wrote in the language of these old folksongs, called Old Scots. He composed original works and also collected many of his mother's folksongs to be published. Because of Burns's efforts, readers can enjoy these old works today.

Robert's father, William, had a very different influence. He was a strict and religious man. He believed in formal education and worked hard to get it for Robert. Unfortunately, Robert could not stay in school for long. The family farm possessed very poor soil, and it was too much work for William alone. In order for their family to survive, Robert had to join his father in the fields. William still tried to continue his son's education, though. As they worked, William talked with Robert and taught him independence. Robert's independent streak can be seen in many of his poems—especially his satires, which are sarcastic works of ridicule. In these poems, Burns mocked politicians, aristocrats, and hypocrites.

By the age of fifteen, Robert had become the chief laborer on the family farm. The experience was a mixed blessing. On one hand, these years of hard labor led to many recurring health problems for Burns as an adult. On the other hand, his experiences led him to write beautiful poems about the countryside. Farm life instilled in him a deep respect for the poorest of people and the lowliest of animals. It was also on the farm that Robert met his first love. In 1774, he fell for a fellow farmhand named Nelly Kirkpatrick. Inspired, he wrote his first song, "O Once I Lov'd." Though he wrote many more love poems during his life, the first remains Burns's most famous.

As Robert became an adult, he spent what little spare time he had writing and socializing. In 1780, he started a debate club in which he and his friends discussed life, politics, and love. Burns also signed up to take a country dancing class. The dance class, however, made Robert's father incredibly upset. William believed dancing to be sinful, and he fought terribly with his son. Their relationship never fully recovered.

Despite the rift, when William fell ill in 1783, it was Robert who stepped in to run the family farm. For over a year, William had been locked in a dispute with the landlord. Though he had won the fight in court, it had cost William his health and all of his family's savings. It was up to Robert to take control. During this stressful time, he wrote his first poetry collection. It was called the *First Commonplace Book*.

William passed away in 1784, and Robert moved his family to a new farm in Mossgiel, Scotland. In Mossgiel, Robert fell in love with a young girl named Jean Armour. In 1786, she became pregnant with twins by Robert, which was quite a scandal. Jean came from a very well-respected family. While Robert had success on his farm, he was anything but respectable. Jean's father did not like his satirical poems, which criticized the church. He refused to let them marry or even visit each other, sending Robert into despair.

Since he could not be with Jean, Robert decided to leave Scotland altogether. He booked passage on a ship to Jamaica, where he could start his life anew. To pay for the trip, he composed a book of poetry to sell, called *Poems, Chiefly in the Scottish Dialect*. While the book's title was not exactly snappy, people quickly recognized the quality of the poems within. One of Scotland's top critics, a man named Blacklock, gave the book a rave review. Also, an aristocrat named Mrs. Dunlop helped to spread the word about Burns's talent. Robert sold every copy of his first printing. A second printing swiftly sold out as well. Suddenly, twenty-seven-year-old Robert Burns went from scandal-plagued farmer to the most famous man in Scotland! In an odd way, had he not had his troubles with Jean's father, Robert might never have reached such heights.

Burns's popularity continued to grow. A third printing of his book carried his poems all through Europe and America. Robert did not let fame change him, though. He remained generous and respectful toward the poets who preceded him. In fact, once he could afford to, Burns bought a headstone for the grave of his favorite poet, Robert Fergusson. It was Burns's way of repaying Fergusson. As he did with all things he valued, Burns made sure that the poet would be remembered.

After a tour of Scotland, Burns returned home and married Jean in 1788. Though famous, he still needed a steady income to support his growing family. So, he returned to the thing he knew best: farming. Unfortunately, Robert had his father's luck when it came to picking land. His farm, Ellisland, was a failure, plagued by poor soil. Instead of providing security, it lost money every year that Burns owned it. The difficult labor also hurt his health. Eventually, Robert called upon rich friends he had made through Mrs. Dunlop. With their help, he found work as an exciseman. It was his job to collect taxes and catch smugglers.

As an exciseman, Robert could finally earn a comfortable salary. He sold Ellisland and moved his family to Dumfries, Scotland. At Dumfries, Burns met Maria Riddell, a young woman who would become a close friend. Maria was also a writer, and Robert helped her to get some of her work published. In a time where men and women were not considered to be equal, Robert saw Maria as his peer.

For several years, it seemed as though Robert had everything he desired. Money was no longer a problem, and in his leisure time, he collected over one hundred old Scots folksongs to be preserved. However, not all was well. Though collecting taxes was less strenuous than farming, the long days of travel on horseback took their toll. Robert's chronic health problems continued to flare up.

In 1795, Robert's health sharply declined. He sought advice from doctors, but they did not have the knowledge to identify his illness. They could not know that Burns's troubles came from a leaky heart valve; the stethoscope had not even been invented yet. Robert grew sicker and sicker, and on July 21, 1796, he passed away.

And with that, the Bard of Scotland was dead at the young age of thirty-seven. Who would tell his story for all to remember? Would it be his wife, Jean? Would it be an admirer, like Mrs. Dunlop? Or would it be his friend and colleague, Maria Riddell? Maria wrote a moving eulogy for the local paper, but she was not chosen to write his full biography. Though Burns thought her to be his equal, others did not believe that a woman was suited to the task. So, a man was chosen. This man was not an "old acquaintance." In fact, he had only met Burns once. As one might guess, this near-stranger, Dr. James Currie, wrote a very inaccurate biography. He edited and destroyed many of Burns's personal letters. He also spread the false rumor that Robert was killed by alcoholism.

Fortunately, Currie's biography was not the final word on Robert Burns. Others who knew Robert personally wrote of him, and more of his letters resurfaced. Decades later, as science advanced, doctors proved the true cause of Burns's death: not idle drinking, but overwork. Today, Currie's falsehoods still persist as part of the Burns legend, but many Burns fans know the truth.

In her eulogy, Maria Riddell wrote about Robert's "irresistible power of attraction." By that, she meant that anyone who read his work could feel close to him, as if they knew him personally. Perhaps this is why every year, people around the world gather on January 25, the day of the poet's birth. They come to eat a traditional Scottish dinner, sing songs, and drink ale—and especially to remember their "old acquaintance," Rabbie Burns.

K-K Gregory: Kid Inventor

by Patricia Bernard
illustrated by Matthew Casper

In 1994, ten-year-old Kathryn (K-K) Gregory was building a fort in the snow. Her wrists got cold and wet, and they started to hurt. To help herself keep warm, she invented Wristies®, which are worn underneath gloves and coats to keep out the wind and cold. She tested them out on her Girl Scout troop, then got a patent and started her own company. She became the youngest person to sell her product on a television shopping show. She also received several awards and other recognitions for her invention.

It was not easy for K-K, however. Some kids made fun of her and her Wristies®. Some adults could not believe that she was an inventor. But K-K didn't give up. She patented her invention and advertised it. She learned all about creating a new product and selling it. She even appeared on television shows to talk about her invention. Today, Wristies, Inc. is a successful company. K-K's mother, Susan Gregory, is its president, while K-K herself is the company's inventor and vice-president.

Frida Kahlo: Spirited Painter

by Sarah Marino
illustrated by Matthew Casper

Frida Kahlo is the most well-known woman artist from Mexico. Her vivid paintings, many of which are self-portraits, reflect much of the pain that she dealt with in her life. They also display her enormous will and perseverance. Frida created a style of painting that was uniquely her own. While it resembles work of the Surrealist artists of the early-twentieth century, she claimed that she was not a Surrealist. She said, "I never painted dreams. I painted my own reality. The only thing I know is that I paint because I need to, and I paint always whatever passes through my head, without any other consideration."

Frida was born in the town of Coyoacán on July 6, 1907, in a house that her father had built. Her father had immigrated to Mexico from Germany in the late 1800s. There, he changed his name from Wilhelm to the more Mexican-sounding Guillermo. He married Frida's mother, who was born in Mexico and had Spanish and

Indian ancestors. Frida had three sisters and two half-sisters from her father's first marriage. Her father was a successful photographer. However, he was rarely home and did not show his daughters a lot of affection.

Just three years after she was born, in 1910, the Mexican Revolution began. For years after, political and social chaos swept through the country. This struggle greatly influenced Frida as she grew up. She was involved in politics throughout her adult life. She often marched at rallies with her husband, the painter Diego Rivera. Indeed, to show her support and her ties to the Revolution, Frida later claimed that she was born in 1910, instead of 1907.

At the age of six, Frida became afflicted with the disease polio. It forced her to spend nine months in bed. When she had healed, her right leg remained very thin and disfigured. Many children made fun of Frida as she tried to regain her physical strength by playing sports and doing other activities. Sadly, this incident was only the first of many physical tragedies to affect Frida throughout her life.

For high school, Frida entered the prestigious National Preparatory School in Mexico City. This school provided an accelerated academic education. It primed students for enrollment in the National University of Mexico, which was nearby. Students at both institutions were taught by Mexico's most renowned scholars and professionals. At the time Frida began attending, the Mexican Revolution was coming to a close and a period of reform had begun. Many old political and social agencies were giving way to freer models of government. These new models aimed to give more power to all Mexicans.

In this atmosphere, Frida became friends with many intelligent and socially active students. Her closest friends formed a group of nine and called themselves the *Cachuchas*, for a kind of hat they wore. One of the boys, Alejandro Arias, became Frida's boyfriend in her later years at the school. Frida was bright and loved to read, and she planned to someday attend medical school. Tragically, this plan changed in mere minutes when an accident upended Frida's life. The accident also began the transformation that would make Frida the brilliant artist whom we know of today.

On September 17, 1925, Frida and Alejandro boarded a bus after school that would take them to Coyoacán. The bus was wooden and not very sturdy. As it rounded a corner, a trolley car hit the bus and smashed it to pieces. Frida suffered tremendously. A bus handrail cut straight through her abdomen. Her spine, collarbone, pelvis, and ribs were broken. Her right leg was fractured and her right foot broken. As Frida wrote later, "A handrail pierced me the way a sword pierces a bull."

Frida spent months in recovery. She suffered pain and additional surgeries for the rest of her life. The accident was also the reason for her early death, at the age of forty-seven. During her recovery, when she was forced to lie and sit still for very long periods, she began

to paint. Her father had painted as a hobby. She studied his art books and copied the techniques used by classic European painters. Frida's first paintings were of her family members and friends, and one self-portrait for Alejandro.

A few years later, once she had recovered enough to be active again, she met Diego Rivera. At the time, he was painting murals in Mexico City. She went to the place where he was painting and boldly asked him for his advice. Since Diego was a very successful, wealthy artist of that time, Frida wanted to know if he thought she had the talent to make a living from her work. She showed him a few of her paintings, and he admired them and encouraged her. The two became friends, and as they spent more time together, love grew between them. They got married on August 21, 1929.

The next year, Diego was commissioned to complete murals in San Francisco, California. The couple moved there and stayed for quite some time. Away from her family and friends, Frida often felt lonely and isolated. She used her painting as a way to keep her mind off of her troubles and, eventually, she made a few close friends.

In 1932, Diego was hired to create murals in Detroit, Michigan, and the couple moved again. Frida's friend was able to stay with her during this time, but Frida still had difficulty. In Detroit, she suffered tremendous pain because of the accident that had happened years earlier, and she learned that she would never be able to have a child. This distressful news caused Frida to give up painting for a time. However, as she had after the accident, Frida summoned her inner will and fortitude. She chose to use painting as a way to express her hurt instead of keeping it inside.

Many scholars feel that in Detroit, Frida's style truly became her own. The paintings she made there showed growth in her skill and creativity. She began to express her pain in such a way that no female artist had ever done before. While some of the images were very bleak, they were truly creative and spoke to Frida's ability to conjure emotions. One can see and understand her pain, but also her strength.

Most of Frida's paintings were self-portraits. She once said, "I paint myself because I am so often alone, because I am the subject I know best." While Frida expressed her own grief in her work, viewers can feel and share in her emotions by studying her paintings. In a way, because her work is so emotional, it can also help people to feel their own sadness and grief, to feel that someone else has experienced such things and persevered despite pain.

After Detroit, Frida and Diego moved to New York, where Diego was hired to paint murals in Rockefeller Center. Due to a political disagreement over the murals, the project was canceled. This made Frida wish to return to Mexico. Diego agreed, although part of him did not want to return to their homeland.

In their next few years in Mexico, the couple endured difficult times and a period apart. Despite their struggles, Diego always supported and admired Frida's painting. They had a strong friendship which supported their marriage and kept them together until Frida's death. During their troubles, Frida again turned to painting as a way to express her feelings and take her mind off of her problems. Her talent continued to grow, and in 1938, she had a solo art show of her paintings in New York City. The following year she went to Paris. There, her work was exhibited alongside artwork by European Surrealist painters. After this show, the famous Louvre museum purchased one of Frida's paintings.

Frida returned to Mexico and continued to paint, even as her health declined. Frida and Diego's friends—artists, writers, social activists, and the like—frequently came to visit. She spent time with her family and had many pets as well. In Mexico, Frida was never as isolated as she had been in America; however, her physical pain persisted and she kept painting it in her art.

In the final years of her life, Frida became an art teacher and continued painting. She was hospitalized for much of the year in 1950. A few years later, she had her first art show in Mexico City. Unfortunately, her health had worsened to a dire state. In 1954, she passed away at the age of forty-seven, dying in the same house in which she had been born.

Frida's life and artwork continue to inspire and serve as an example of the power of human will. Despite the enormous tragedy and hardships of her life, Frida found a way to continue on and thrive. She worked, married, traveled, enjoyed many friends and companions, and painted her pain with creativity and beauty.

The Lady in Charge

by Debbie Parrish
illustrated by Dave Rushbrook

The "Angel of the Battlefield" and the "Lady in Charge"—both are names given to one of the most important women in American history. Clarissa Harlowe Barton was born on December 25, 1821, in North Oxford, Massachusetts. She was quick to let everyone know that she preferred to be called Clara. This is only a small example of how well she knew her own mind and took charge of her life. She used that strength to make a tremendous difference in the world. Clara Barton has been widely honored for her humanitarian efforts. Humanitarian efforts are those made to improve the lives of others. She was also admired for her pioneer spirit. It helped her to lead the way for women in many areas.

Clara Barton had a natural gift for learning. By the age of four, she could already spell three-syllable words. Clara was taught at home by her brothers and sisters. She received a diverse education from them. At age eleven, Miss Barton showed an aptitude for nursing. That is when she cared for her brother David, who had a very serious illness. At only seventeen years old, Clara Barton became a teacher in Massachusetts. This was at a time when most teachers were men. Six years later, she furthered her education at the Liberal Institute in Clinton, New York. After studying languages and writing, she moved to New Jersey. There, she opened a free school of her own. It was highly successful. However, at the age of thirty-five, she left the teaching profession. She resigned when a man was named headmaster instead of her.

Upon leaving teaching, Clara moved into government work. She became the first female clerk in the US Patent Office. In fact, she was the first woman to receive such a clerkship in any government office. For a time, Barton received the same pay as male clerks. Men who were against women working in these offices eventually managed to have her job reduced to "copyist." In 1857, her job was eliminated completely. In 1860, however, Clara Barton returned to the office as a temporary copyist. She was never easily discouraged.

Clara Barton is famous for being first in many areas. In 1861, at the start of the Civil War, she became the first woman to be allowed in wartime hospitals and camps, and on the battlefields. She earned this freedom by gaining the trust of military officials. Nine days after the Civil War began, a trainload of dead and wounded soldiers arrived in Washington, DC, without supplies. Clara Barton tended to the soldiers. She arranged for supplies and their medical needs. This helped her understand a critical need. She had found a new way to be of service to others.

After the first Battle of Bull Run, Barton helped establish an agency that gathered and distributed supplies for wounded soldiers. Clara proved that she was extremely capable. She rode in ambulances, delivering care to wounded soldiers. After begging people in charge, Clara Barton was given permission to travel to the front lines of battle. She gathered medical supplies from all over the country and took them to the battlefields. She worked tirelessly to help the battle-worn soldiers. She called these soldiers "her boys." In turn, the soldiers called her the "Angel of the Battlefield."

In 1864, Barton was named the superintendent of Union nurses. She arranged for hospital supplies, camp needs, military trains, and battlefield medical personnel. Union General Benjamin Butler often called her the "Lady in Charge." All the while, Clara Barton refused to accept any pay from the government.

When the war ended, Clara Barton saw another human need. She had become extremely concerned about missing soldiers. President Abraham Lincoln allowed her access to the US Office of Correspondence. This office had files on the letters sent between families and soldiers. She began a letter writing campaign to search for missing soldiers. She also traveled to Camp Parole, Maryland. There, she organized a program for finding men listed as "missing in action." Barton and her assistants were able to identify over twenty-two thousand missing soldiers.

Barton's last Civil War-related act of humanitarianism was to insist upon a national cemetery. This final resting place was created at the site of the Andersonville Prison in Georgia. Thousands of Union soldiers had died and been buried there while being held as prisoners of war. Former soldier and prisoner Dorence Atwater had secretly kept a list of names of soldiers who were dying in the camp while he was imprisoned. With the help of Atwater and other military personnel, Clara Barton was able to identify and mark over thirteen thousand graves of Union soldiers. She also suggested that a memorial be built for unidentified soldiers. This accomplishment was another first. It was a model for our country's present Tomb of the Unknown Soldier in Arlington National Cemetery near Washington, DC.

Clara Barton felt satisfied with her contributions during the war. She traveled to Europe in 1869 to rest.

However, she had not left her interest in public service behind. While visiting Geneva, Switzerland, she learned of a group called the Red Cross. Barton read a book written by Henry Dunant, the organization's founder. She became more and more interested in the Red Cross Movement.

The Red Cross wanted international agreements to protect and care for the sick and injured during wartime. They wanted to do this without respect to nationality. The Red Cross aimed to create national groups of volunteers to give help on a neutral basis. At the Geneva Convention in 1864, this idea was accepted by twelve European countries. It is often referred to as the Geneva Treaty or the Red Cross Treaty.

When war broke out in Europe in 1870, Clara Barton was not yet a member of the Red Cross. She made herself a cross from red ribbons and sewed it on her clothes anyway. On the battlefields, she helped the wounded and filled needs however she could. In France, she helped deliver supplies to those in need. While doing this, she realized that French citizens affected by the war were in need of clothing. Seeing this, she opened workrooms to sew new clothes to meet those needs.

Clara Barton was motivated by all she had learned and her experiences in Europe. She came home excited to bring the Red Cross to the United States. This was no easy task. She faced many problems in getting others to agree with her proposals. In 1877, the first president she approached, Rutherford B. Hayes, refused to consider her request. He claimed the United States's becoming a part of the Geneva Treaty would be an "entangling alliance." True to her pioneer spirit, Clara Barton did not give up. The next president, James Garfield, liked the treaty, but he was assassinated before he could sign it. Again, Clara Barton did not give up. Finally, in 1882, President Chester A. Arthur signed the Geneva Treaty.

In 1881, a group in Washington, DC, organized the first Red Cross in the United States. The group chose Clara Barton as its leader. They called themselves the American Association of the Red Cross. After Congress approved the Geneva Treaty, the group reorganized. In 1883, they became the American National Red Cross. The United States Congress gave charters to the group in 1900 and again in 1905. Today's American Red Cross has an ongoing working relationship with the federal government. It is no surprise that the first head of the American Red Cross was none other than Clara Barton.

The Red Cross grew under Barton's leadership. They began to give aid in peace time disasters. The Red Cross assisted citizens hurt by the floods of the Mississippi and Ohio Rivers in 1882 and 1884. When the Texas famine of 1886 and the Florida yellow fever epidemic in 1887 overcame many Americans, the Red Cross came to help. After the Illinois earthquake of 1888 and the Johnstown, Pennsylvania, dam break disaster of 1889, the Red Cross was at their service. The last relief operation in which Barton was personally involved took place in 1900. In that year, she helped to provide money and supplies to Galveston, Texas. Here, over six thousand people had lost their lives and many others had lost their homes in a hurricane and tidal wave disaster.

Inspired by the ideas of its founder, Clara Barton had taken a wonderful organization and expanded upon its humanitarian ideals. Other countries wanted to change their Red Cross organizations to include disaster relief as well. In 1884, the American Amendment was added to the Geneva Treaty. It included disaster relief internationally. This earned America the honor of being called the "Good Samaritan of Nations."

Clara Barton served as president of the American National Red Cross for twenty-two years. Never once did she accept money for her services. In 1904, after criticism of her age and management style, Barton resigned from the organization she had created. However, she did not stay idle for long. Barton immediately worked to organize the National First Aid Association. This group encouraged the development of first aid kits. She also developed educational materials to teach first aid skills. She served as honorary president of this organization for five years. Eventually, this organization dissolved, and the Red Cross incorporated first aid into its own programs of health and safety. This was also an idea first proposed by its former leader, Clara Barton.

Clara Barton is best remembered for her humanitarian acts and for bringing the Red Cross to America. She had many other interests as well, however. She remained quite interested in youth education. Whenever possible, she supported prison reform and civil rights. Barton met black activist Frederick Douglas and spoke for black civil rights as she delivered speeches around the country about her Civil War experiences. She was especially noted for her work in the area of women's suffrage, or voting rights for women. Barton became a longtime supporter of Susan B. Anthony, one of the leaders of the women's voting rights movement.

On April 12, 1912, in Glen Echo, Maryland, Clara Barton died from complications of a cold. At the age of ninety, the "Lady in Charge" passed away, but her spirit lives on through the work of the American Red Cross. With the casting of every woman's vote in an election or any advancement in civil rights issues, people can reflect upon her pioneer spirit and dedication to improving the lives of all human beings.

Mary McLeod Bethune: American Educator

by Jill Fisher
illustrated by Dave Rushbrook

"We live in a world which respects power above all things. Power, intelligently directed, can lead to more freedom."
— *Mary McLeod Bethune*

Mary McLeod was born on July 10, 1875. She was the fifteenth of seventeen children. However, she was the first free child born in her family. Her parents, Samuel and Patsy McLeod, were farmers. Before the Civil War, they were slaves. Once the war was over, the Thirteenth Amendment of the Constitution of the United States abolished slavery. Sadly, many of Mary's brothers and sisters had already been sold into slavery. It had happened right before their parents' eyes.

Even after Samuel and Patsy were free, they continued to work for their former master until they could afford to buy land of their own. They built a three-room log cabin on their five acres of land, which they called "The Homestead." It was in Mayesvile, South Carolina.

Mary's parents taught her the value of hard work and dedication. At the age of only five years old, Mary started to work in the cotton fields. She helped by planting, weeding, and picking cotton. She also worked part time doing laundry with her mother for white families. Sometimes she waited for her mother to deliver clean clothes to homes. As she waited, she would play with the owner's granddaughter. She noticed a book and a doll. As she reached to play with the book, the white child grabbed it away and said, "Put that book down. You can't read! You're black!" It was then that Mary realized how much she desired to read. She decided that she would learn how because it meant freedom and success in life. The only problem was that there were almost no black teachers or schools in Mayesville.

Soon, a woman named Emma Wilson opened a school for African-American children in Mayesville. It was called Presbyterian Mission School. Despite their struggles, Mary's parents allowed her to attend the school. Even though she had to walk five miles each way to school and the equipment was old, she was happy to learn reading, writing, arithmetic, and new music. After a while, Mary began to share her new knowledge with her family. Once she graduated, she went back to working in the fields. She really wished to further her education, though.

"From the first, I made my learning, what little it was, useful every way I could."

— *Mary McLeod Bethune*

It didn't take long for Mary's wish to come true. Mary Crissman, a Quaker seamstress from Colorado, wanted to help give a black girl an education. She did not know into whom she was investing scholarship money, but she requested it be a girl who would do well.

Now that Mary's education was paid for, she could attend Scotia Seminary in North Carolina. She was very impressed with the luxuries, such as rooming with only one girl, and eating with table clothes and silverware. Mary liked the way black and white teachers worked together. She was quoted as saying, "The white teachers taught that the color of a person's skin has nothing to do with his brains—and color, caste, and class distinction are evil."

Mary went on to attend the Moody Bible Institute in Chicago, Illinois. It was a very different experience than Scotia Seminary. She was the only black student at her new school. She was often treated poorly because of her skin color. This treatment changed Mary. She was no longer afraid to stand up for herself and her rights. She was very proud of everything she had accomplished so far in her life.

When Mary was a little girl, she used to listen to her grandma's stories. They were about Africa and the Bible. The stories caught Mary's attention. When she thought of them, they made her want to become a missionary to help people in Africa. However, her application to do so was denied because of her race. Mary said this was the greatest disappointment of her life. So, she returned home, not knowing what she would do next.

"Invest in a human soul...it might be a diamond in the rough."

– Mary McLeod Bethune

Not long after she returned home to the South, Mary began her career as a teacher. As she taught, she realized that her desire to do missionary work could be used at home. Mary worked with Emma Wilson, her first teacher, for a time. She then taught at the Haines Institute in Georgia for many years. This was a private school for African-American children. Next she moved to North Carolina and taught at the Kendall Institute. That is where she met Alburtus Bethune, a fellow teacher.

Mary and Alburtus got married and moved to Georgia. They had a son, Albert. Mary often dreamed of opening her own school. She knew schools were needed in Florida due to the growing black population. So she moved to Daytona, Florida, to fulfill her dream. Alburtus did not share her dream. He refused to move and they went their separate ways.

"The whole world opened to me when I learned to read."

– Mary McLeod Bethune

It only took a small amount of money to start Mary's dream. She found an old two-story house that was available for rent. She paid fifty cents for the down payment and eleven dollars rent each month. Starting a school was hard work. Mary often looked through the garbage for things that could be used in her school. She found old furniture, lamps, and other supplies. She sold sweet potato pies to make money. Mary rode her old bike to look for African-American girls to attend her school.

Finally, the Industrial Institute for Negro Girls opened. There were six students: five girls and Mary's son, Albert. The students raised money for the school by selling baked goods and singing for donations. It did not take long for the school to grow.

"Studying goes deeper than mere reading. There are surface nuggets to be gathered but the best of the gold is underneath, and it takes time and labor to secure it."
– Mary McLeod Bethune

In only two years, the school grew to have two hundred fifty students and four teachers. Adults attended night classes to learn how to read, write, and do arithmetic. More rooms and supplies were needed as the school grew. Mary collected donations and was able to buy new land on which she built a second school. It was an all-boy African-American school. With the Industrial Institute for Negro Girls, the Bethune-Cookman College was formed. It still exists today.

Mary McLeod Bethune was not only a dedicated teacher. She was also a powerful activist. As she ran the school, she also started a hospital for black people until public ones opened their services to them. Mary became a voice on behalf of both women and African-Americans. She became involved in organizations that tried to improve the lives of black people and women.

President Franklin D. Roosevelt often relied on Mary's knowledge and wisdom. He named her the Director of Negro Affairs for the National Youth Administration. They found employment for young black people during the Great Depression, a time when money was most scarce all across the world. This was the highest government position held by a woman.

Mary McLeod Bethune continued to help others until her death. She died on May 18, 1955. Mary had a positive impact on the lives of many blacks and women. Because of her hard work, she was honored with a postage stamp in her name thirty years after her death.

"I leave you love…hope…the challenge of developing confidence in each other…a thirst for education…a respect for the use of power…faith…racial dignity…a desire to live harmoniously with your fellow men. I leave you, finally, a responsibility to our young people."

–Mary McLeod Bethune

George Washington Carver: Scholar, Scientist, Inventor

by Patricia Bernard
illustrated by Kent Kerr

Some people grow up with a strong wish to make the world a better place. George Washington Carver was that kind of person. Carver was a sickly baby, born to slave parents in Missouri during the Civil War. By the time he died, he had become a famous, well-educated man who made many important contributions to his country. Amazingly, George Washington Carver grew up without bitterness for his poverty or for the prejudice he had experienced.

After Carver lost his mother, he lived with the people she had worked for. Because he was frail, Carver did not have to do heavy chores. Instead, he spent time outdoors, exploring nature. He was interested in plants and other living things. He became good at caring for the flowers around his home. Carver could help sick plants get well. He also liked doing experiments, learning how sunlight, water, and different soils affected plants.

Carver loved to learn and study. He eventually passed an exam to get into a college in Kansas. When the school officials found out that he was African-American, though, they refused to let him come to the college. They were prejudiced, which was sadly quite common at that time. Six years later, Carver was finally able to get into Iowa Agricultural College, and in 1894, he became the first African-American to graduate from that college. He was hired by the college as a botanist and continued his studies of plants and plant diseases. He got a master's degree in 1896. Booker T. Washington, another famous African-American, hired him to direct agricultural research, or the study of farming, at Tuskegee Institute.

George Washington Carver worked for the rest of his life to learn more about plant products and to help poor farmers. Bad soil and pests like the boll weevil damaged cotton and made it hard for farmers who depended on their cotton crops. Carver found hundreds of uses for other crops: peanuts, soybeans, and sweet potatoes. He made plastics, ink, vinegar, oils, rubber, and many other products from these plants. These new crops could all be grown in the southern United States. His discoveries made it possible for farmers to grow and sell more kinds of crops in the South. After Carver's work, the South grew four times more peanut crops than it had been growing!

Carver also taught people how to grow vegetables and how to cook food that was inexpensive but nutritious. He wrote a paper on growing tomatoes as well as recipes for cooking them. These recipes included stewed, stuffed, breaded, broiled, and baked tomatoes. There were directions for tomato soup, catsup, and goulash, tomatoes fried, curried, panned, and puréed (cooked and strained). He wrote 115 recipes for preparing tomatoes! He did the same for peanuts. He also created many products made from peanuts, from food items to paints and gasoline.

As an African-American, Mr. Carver helped break down the walls of prejudice. In 1920, he was invited to speak to the American Congress. This was very unusual since the country was very segregated at the time, and African-Americans and whites were not treated with equal respect. Because of his intelligence, courtesy, and hard work, however, George Washington Carver became well-known and well-respected. He did not only research plants; he mentored children, wrote poetry, and painted. He also met with three presidents: Theodore Roosevelt, Calvin Coolidge, and Franklin Roosevelt.

Though he received many honors and awards for his work, Carver himself was not very interested in money or fame. His goal was to help poor farmers, especially black farmers. In 1940, he gave Tuskegee Institute the money he had saved during his lifetime so that it could create scholarships in natural science. He still wanted to contribute to the world, his country, and his people. He lived his life according to those values, and on his grave it is written:

"He could have added fortune to fame, but caring for neither, he found happiness and honor in being helpful to the world."

Roberto Clemente, Baseball Hero

by Michael Scotto
illustrated by Dion Williams

The average career of a baseball player lasts seven years. With the Pittsburgh Pirates, Roberto Clemente played for eighteen years, from 1955 – 1972. During most of his career, he was not the most famous of players. He often felt underappreciated, and as a black Latino player, he faced much prejudice. Today, though, Roberto is known as one of the greatest to ever pick up a bat. He is also one of the most loved.

Roberto Clemente Walker was born on August 18, 1934. He was the youngest of seven children. His family lived in Puerto Rico, in a town called Carolina. Roberto played baseball in his spare time from a very young age. His family was very poor, so he could not always use a bat and ball. When he could not, he would happily use a soup can and a stick to practice. He would practice whenever he could, for as long as he could. In fact, as a boy, his nickname was "Momen" because he was always telling his family "*momentito, momentito.*" *Momentito* is a way of saying "give me another moment" in Spanish.

Roberto played his whole Major League career for the Pittsburgh Pirates. But it was another team that first discovered him: the Brooklyn Dodgers. A scout for the Dodgers had seen him play in Puerto Rico when he was eighteen years old. The scout was very impressed, and the Dodgers gave Clemente a contract one year later. He played for their Minor League team, the Montreal Royals. He was the youngest player on the team.

Roberto felt underappreciated with the Royals. In his first game as a Royal, he pulled off the very rare feat of hitting an in-the-park home run. However, the Royals did not let him play very often. Part of the reason that Clemente got passed over was due to prejudice. He was black and Hispanic, which was a rare combination in baseball at the time. But the Dodgers were also worried that if other teams saw how talented he was, they would offer him more money and he would leave.

Even though the Dodgers tried to hide Roberto, he was still noticed. At the end of every season, the Major League teams held a draft. The team with the worst record got to have the first pick. That year, the worst team was the Pittsburgh Pirates. They could have picked any player they wanted, but they chose Roberto Clemente. In the 1950s, the Pirates team was thought of as sort of a joke in baseball. They hoped that Clemente would be the player to help them turn the team around. In turn, Clemente hoped that with this new team, his talent would finally be recognized.

Clemente's start with the Pirates, though, was somewhat rocky. Roberto had a hard time adjusting to his new home. Blacks were treated quite differently in the United States than they were in Puerto Rico. Some whites in Pittsburgh still did not want black or foreign players on their team. Roberto was accepted by the African-American community in Pittsburgh, but even there, he still felt distant because he came from a different culture. He felt very lonely away from his family. Luckily, though, he rented a room from a very kind African-American couple who helped him. Their names were Stanley and Mamie Garland, and over time, Roberto grew to think of them as his "American parents."

Roberto also suffered several injuries during his first season. When he did play, though, he dazzled the crowds with his determination and unique style. He took a long time to prepare each time he was up at bat. He took time to stretch his neck, which often hurt because of how hard he played. He also was picky about which bat he would use and how the dirt was arranged in the batter's box. He would sometimes tell the umpire "*momentito*" as he prepared. It made pitchers nervous as they waited, but the fans enjoyed the show. The fans were Roberto's favorite part of being a professional ball player. They always gave him comfort when he felt lonesome or homesick.

Still, the early years were a time of frustration. Roberto wanted desperately to show everyone his greatness, perhaps too desperately. He had an incredibly powerful throwing arm, but sometimes he would make wild throws. He also had several more injuries that slowed him down. However, he continued to improve, and so did the Pirates. By the end of the 1950s, the team was finally winning more games than it was losing, something it had not done since before World War II.

In the first game of 1960, Roberto Clemente led the way to a Pirates win. He batted in five runs, hitting two doubles and a single. The Pirates started out on top, and remained number one for almost the whole season. Just like in the first game, Roberto led the way all season. He finished first in the league in runs produced, and his play in the outfield was much improved as well. Unfortunately, no local sports writers spoke Spanish, and many avoided Clemente when it came time to write their stories. Roberto was a humble man, but he always spoke out when he felt disrespected. That did not win him many fans in the press, either.

That year, the Pirates reached the World Series. They faced the great New York Yankees. Most believed that the Pirates were outmatched, and in three games, it seemed like they were. The Pirates lost games two, three, and six by a total of 38 – 3. But these underdogs eventually won the World Series, four games to three. Roberto Clemente hit safely in all seven games, and he was the only player on either team to do so.

After the championship, Roberto skipped the team parties and went home to his family in Puerto Rico. With the bonus money he got from the World Series, he bought his mother a house. His family was the only group more important to him than his fans. In a way, though, Roberto brought the fans home with him, too. Roberto had won a trophy for being the fans' favorite player, and he brought that home to Carolina.

Roberto may have been the fans' favorite, but among the sports writers he did not do so well. Every year, the nation's sports writers voted to choose the Major League's Most Valuable Player. Even though Roberto was the most outstanding player on the best team in baseball, he only came in eighth place. Roberto took it as an insult—one that he would not forget for the rest of his career.

For the rest of the 1960s, the Pirates struggled to match their World Series success. However, as the Pirates sunk, Roberto soared. He was fired up. Losing the MVP award had given him more drive to be great than ever. He won awards as the best hitter and right fielder. He was also invited to play in baseball's All-Star game nearly every year.

In between seasons with the Pirates, Roberto returned home to Carolina. He played baseball with a Puerto Rican professional team during the winters. During a winter season in 1963, Roberto met a woman named Vera Zabala at a drug store. He fell for her right away. He asked everyone he could about her. He even asked the druggist if he could help set them up on a date. Vera's father was very strict, and he set up a schedule of when Roberto could visit her. Vera did not understand why a famous baseball player was so interested in her. She also did not see why Roberto wanted to move so quickly in their relationship. For a man whose nickname had been "Momen"—for *momentito*—it seemed strange. When she asked Roberto about it, he said that life was a fever, no time to waste. Though he took his time up at bat, Roberto lived the rest of his life in a rush.

The next year, Roberto brought Vera to the United States. He introduced her to his "American parents," the Garlands. When Vera saw the way Roberto treated Mrs. Garland, she lost all of her doubts. The two were married in Carolina on November 11, 1964.

As the 1960s continued, Roberto seemed to become more comfortable. He frequently felt misunderstood, but his skill at communicating in English was improving. In 1966, he won the award he felt he deserved back in 1960: the MVP. The recognition made him feel less bitter. He also began to talk more of things beyond baseball. One of Roberto's dreams was to build a sports city in Puerto Rico, where all children, no matter how poor, could go and learn.

Roberto also talked more about civil rights. Martin Luther King, Jr., was one of Clemente's heroes. When King was killed in 1968, many players wanted to delay the start of the season until after his funeral. Roberto led the way in that effort, and, eventually, the league agreed to push its opening day back to show respect.

In 1971, the Pirates found themselves once again on top of the league. They were back in a familiar position. They had made it to the World Series and were the underdogs again. They were not facing the New York Yankees this time, but rather the Baltimore Orioles. Roberto was no longer a young player, either. He was thirty-seven years old. In regular life, that was young, but for a professional ball player, thirty-seven was nearly ancient. He had played for the Pirates for almost half of his life.

It was impossible to tell Roberto's age from his play, though. Just like in 1960, he hit safely in every game, and was the star player of the series. What was different, though, was that this time, everyone took notice. Sports writers described his play as being "near perfection." It was the recognition that Clemente had always hoped for. After the Pirates won the Series, Roberto told the press, "For the first time, I have no regrets."

In 1972, Roberto Clemente did not play as often as he did in previous years. Out of 162 games, he played in only 102. He spent more time sharing his wisdom with the team's young players. When Roberto did play, though, he played extremely well. Just before the season ended, he got his three thousandth hit, a double that hit the left field wall. He was only the eleventh player to reach the three thousand mark. In that game, he also tied the record for most games played by a Pirate. He appeared very briefly in one more game so that he could break the record.

The Pirates were knocked out of the playoffs that year in the first round. Most players look to the off-season as a chance to rest and heal from injuries. But as usual, Roberto kept himself very busy. He arranged baseball clinics for poor Puerto Rican children. He organized a celebration for Bob Prince, the Pirates radio announcer. Unlike many journalists, Prince had always treated Roberto with fairness and respect. He wanted to return the favor by hosting a parade in Carolina.

Lastly, Roberto had another baseball job. The amateur World Championship was coming up in Nicaragua, and he was asked to join the Puerto Rican team. He would not be a player, though; he was to be the manager.

Roberto grew very fond of Nicaragua while he was there. Every morning, he took pocketsful of coins and gave them to poor villagers near his hotel. He learned about their lives, their homes, and their families. He also visited hospitals. At one, he met a boy named Julio who had lost his legs in an accident. With some help, Roberto raised money for Julio to get a pair of prosthetic legs. He promised Julio that he could be the batboy in the following year's baseball tournament.

Even though his team did not win the tournament, Roberto was excited to coach again the next year. He was excited to return to the Pirates as well. Over his long career, he had won four titles for having the best batting record and twelve awards for his play in the outfield, but he was eager to achieve even more. First, though, he looked forward to a joyful Christmas and New Year holiday with his family in Carolina.

Just before Christmas, though, Roberto heard terrible news. There had been a large earthquake in Nicaragua. The quake had destroyed over three hundred fifty square blocks and the town where he had stayed was destroyed. There were thousands of people missing, and hundreds of thousands were homeless. It was hard to get much direct information about the tragedy, but Roberto felt so close to the people he had met in Nicaragua that he immediately sprang into action.

Within days, Clemente put together a committee to work on helping the Nicaraguans. He arranged three airplane flights to transport supplies for those in need. He raised money in Puerto Rico and helped to gather food, medical supplies, and even an x-ray machine. He wound up gathering much more than he could send down in only three trips. The first planes that traveled to Nicaragua ran into serious trouble. It was chaos in the country. The soldiers and the leader of Nicaragua were doing awful things. They were stealing the supplies that were meant for the people and locking them up for themselves.

When Roberto heard about the stealing, he became very angry. He decided to fly down himself with the next load of supplies. He had to make sure the supplies got to the people who needed them. He arranged another flight at the last minute on New Year's Eve. The plane he got, though, was badly in need of repair. It was also overloaded with supplies. On top of that, the pilot and owner of the plane both had many safety violations that Roberto did not know about. Had he had more time or not been so desperate to help—had he just thought, "*momentito*," as he so often did up at bat—Roberto might have noticed the plane's problems. Sadly, he did not. The plane struggled to take off, and it crashed into the ocean barely after it left Puerto Rico. No one survived, and Roberto's body was never found.

Soon after the crash, Roberto got one final, rare baseball honor. To enter the Baseball Hall of Fame, there was usually a lengthy wait. Before there could even be a vote, a player had to be retired for at least five years. For Roberto, though, the league made an exception and voted him in within three months. It was fitting to rush Clemente in because that was how he lived his life—in a rush to succeed, in a rush to help others find success. Because of his skill and his great heart, today there are forty public schools, two hospitals, and over two hundred parks and baseball fields named for him.

The year before he died, Roberto Clemente gave a speech about human rights. In his speech, he said, "If you have a chance to accomplish something that will make things better for people coming behind you, and you don't do that, you are wasting your time on this earth." While it is tragic that Clemente died so young, with so much promise, it could never be said that he wasted any time.

Interview with Michael Scotto

by Jill Fisher
illustrated by Matthew Casper

*M*ichael Scotto is the author of children's novels, *including the Latasha Gandy books and Postcards from Pismo, as well as the Tales of Midlandia picture book series. He sat down with interviewer Jill Fisher to discuss his life and his craft.*

Jill Fisher: Thanks for joining me, Michael.

Michael Scotto: It's my pleasure!

Let's begin by talking about your background. Where are you from?

I think of Pittsburgh, PA, as my "adopted hometown." I grew up here from age eleven on, and I think of it as my home. Before that I lived in a small city called Middletown, in New York.

Tell me about your education.

I went to public school growing up, and then for college I went to Carnegie Mellon University in Pittsburgh. They have a terrific English department and Creative Writing program, and a great Drama School, so I studied at both. I learned a whole lot about writing, and I ended up getting three degrees while I was there.

Were you always good at writing?

I was always good at describing things. But that's only one part of writing a good story. It took a lot of hard work and practice to become the writer I am today.

Do you recall how your interest in writing started?

Definitely. When I was young, my parents read to me a lot. I also started to read on my own at a very young age. I remember being unhappy when stories I liked

ended, because I wanted to know what happened next. So I started to just imagine what happened next and write it down. Those were my very first stories.

When did you first consider yourself an author?

When I was about seven or eight, I started to write original stories. I would print them off the computer, staple copies together, and give them out to people at school. The process I have to get my work out now is a little different, but I think that's when I really got my first taste of what it's like to be an author.

Do you see writing as a career?

Oh, definitely. There were a few things I could have chosen to do for work. I had a chance to study computer science; I could have studied music. But writing was the only thing that I believed I'd never get tired of.

Are the stories you write based on someone you know or events in your own life?

Sometimes I take little bits here and there. Usually, though, the things that I go through and hear about in real life end up just being a jumping off point. That was definitely true for my first novel, *Latasha and the Little Red Tornado*.

What inspired you to write *Latasha*?

I had a few different inspirations. I wanted to write a book set in Pittsburgh, because it's my city and I love living here. Also, not long before I started writing, I got a puppy that was very energetic and always getting into trouble. I wanted to write about what that was like, so that's where the "little red tornado" came from. The one in the book is even worse-behaved than my dog, though.

I like your title, *Latasha and the Little Red Tornado*. How do you come up with a title?

That's a good question. For *Latasha*, it was the very last thing I wrote. It didn't have a title until the very end. I like my titles to be specific and memorable, so I often take them right from the book. A character calls the dog in *Latasha* a "little red tornado," and I just liked the sound of it. If I have two title ideas to choose between, I say them both aloud, and whichever one sounds better out loud, that's the one I pick.

Who designs the covers for your books?

I can't draw at all, so I'm very lucky to work with a handful of talented illustrators. For example, *Latasha and the Little Red Tornado* was illustrated by Evette Gabriel Villella, who also did the cover art.

What do you do when you are not writing?

I like to take photographs and I like to cook. I spend a lot of time fixing up my house, because it's very old. And, of course, I read all the time.

What genre of books do you like to read? Do you limit yourself to only the genre that you write yourself?

I love children's books, but I read all kinds. I read stuff about politics, and history, and fiction for adults and teens. Basically, if you tell me you liked a book, I'll look it up and give it a shot.

Do you have a specific writing style?

I don't think I do. I like to write lots of different kinds of things. It all depends on what would work best with the story I want to tell. One thing I do write more than anything else is realistic fiction.

How much of what happens in your books is realistic?

Hopefully all of it is believable. I want any kids who read my work to feel a connection to it, like it could happen to them or to someone they know.

What was the hardest part of writing your book?

The hardest part was the ending. I don't want to spoil how the book ends, but it gets kind of dramatic in the last few chapters, and it was tough to write. I didn't want anything bad to happen, because I liked my characters, but at the same time, I wanted to be true to the story.

Did you learn anything from writing your book, and what was it?

I learn something from everything I write. One way I learn is through research while I'm working. In *Latasha*, I did research about National Book Month, and I learned a bit about what it was and what it meant.

If you had to do it all over again, would you change anything in your latest book?

Actually, I don't think so. I'm not saying that the book

is perfect, but I'm very proud of it and I like it just as it is.

What books have influenced your life most?

That is a very hard question! [*laughs*] I'll pick out one book from very early on in my life. That book is *Cloudy with a Chance of Meatballs*. That was one of the first books where I finished it and thought, "I really wish this story kept going!" That feeling is what pushed me down the path to being a writer.

How do you start developing a new story? How do you get inspired for it?

I do a lot of brainstorming. I think about the characters I want to write before I think about the plot. The characters and the choices they make are what lead to the plot. I get inspired by people I see, true stories I read about—it comes from all over.

What is your writing process? Do you follow a regular routine?

The only thing that is consistent from day to day is that I take time to sit down and write. I write nearly every single day, even if I don't especially feel like it.

What advice would you give to people who "run out of creativity" when writing?

If you feel like your story is at a dead end, try writing a little of something else for a bit. Write a short poem, or even write about how you're frustrated that you're stuck!

Do you ever suffer from writer's block? If so, what do you do about it?

I think every writer has good days and bad days. When I'm having a tough time moving forward, I go back to my character sketches. I think about why I want to be writing this story, why it's important to me. Sometimes,

I summarize what I've already written. Going over it a second time can be helpful to finding the next step.

Is there anything you find particularly challenging in your writing?

It can be a challenge to come up with new ideas that are completely original. There have been many times where I came up with an idea I loved, but then I realized another writer had done something very similar before.

Do you have any advice for other writers?

Sure I do. My two main pieces of advice are to read as much as you can, and to practice your writing every day. It can be hard to write something creative every day, but I've learned the most about how to write well from just trying to do it, over and over.

Do you have anything specific that you want to say to your readers?

Keep on reading! (And not just my books!)

Who is your favorite author and what is it that really strikes you about his or her work?

I've always been a big fan of Roald Dahl, who wrote *James and the Giant Peach*, *Charlie and the Chocolate Factory*, and plenty of other terrific books. He writes with such humor. His work is terrifically entertaining.

What are your current projects?

It will probably be different by the time this article is printed, but right now, I am working on a sequel to my first novel, about Latasha Gandy and her family. I'm very excited about it!

Thank you for taking the time to answer all of my questions.

Thanks for having me!

Night Owl

At the Bluebirds' Nest

by Sarah Marino
illustrated by Dion Williams

It's a crisp fall morning on a farm just outside of Nashville. You might expect the home of country rock stars to be extravagant and enormous. This scene paints a different picture, although a stunning one: a three-story stone farmhouse surrounded by lush rolling hills of grassland and small trees and shrubs, along with two large red barns, one of which serves as a makeshift recording studio. The brother and sister who live here, with their parents, are two of the four members of the popular country-rock band the Bluebirds. They recently came home from a tour and are preparing to record some songs that were written while on the road.

We walk into the barn studio, where Chris Canton immediately picks up a guitar and starts playing. "One of the new songs," he explains, strumming quickly. It's a

nice tune. Chris, at eighteen, is the older of the siblings in the group. Lily, his sister, is the band's youngest member at sixteen.

"Who wrote that one?" I ask.

"Miller and I, with some help from Lily on lyrics," he says. Chris is tall and lanky and his light brown hair is spiky and unruly this morning. He wears jeans, a dark green t-shirt, and sandals.

Chris is the main songwriter in the band, although Lily often adds refrains or harmonies to improve songs. The other band mates, Miller Santiago and Paul Reynolds, also help to write the music. Crucial to the writing is their producer, Jay Barnes, who arranges and writes for them and helps them to acquire good songs by other musicians. (In fact, their hit single from 2011, "Night Owl," was written by the lead singer of My Morning Jacket, Jim James.) Their parents have even helped with lyrics at times.

Lily sits at the piano and starts playing some chords. Her wavy, caramel-colored hair is neatly tucked beneath a straw hat. (Lily often wears hats or scarves onstage; it's been said that she has around fifty hats.) They offer to play something for me, a new song they'll be recording soon, called "Fault Line." Chris sits down at the drums (he plays guitar, drums, and piano), and Lily plays the first notes. They both sing. The song begins quietly but picks up momentum in the refrain and builds rhythm and volume to the end. It's played very well. They tell me they've been practicing a lot lately.

When the song is over, I ask them to tell me how it started. Because they're still teenagers, many fans, critics, and reporters are impressed by their level of skill. "How did you learn? How long have you been playing?" I ask.

"All of us have been playing music since we were kids," Chris says, "but I guess Lily and I have been playing professionally for the longest. Both of our parents are musicians." Their father, Ray, plays in a jazz band and teaches at Vanderbilt. Their mother, Tamara, has sung and played piano with several bands in many clubs throughout Nashville.

"We were strongly encouraged," Lily begins, but Chris cuts her off.

"We were forced, basically," he says. They both laugh.

Lily continues. "Yeah, early on we were told to find an instrument we liked. I wanted to start with the fiddle, but we both ended up starting on piano. We had one and Mom was a good pianist, so it was basically a part of our lives like family meals: wake up, breakfast, school, piano, homework, dinner, and more piano."

Chris took to the guitar at age ten, and then drums at fifteen. Lily quit playing for a few years, but eventually picked it back up again at age thirteen, when their father organized a band for them with some family friends. The young group played at churches, private parties, and some restaurants in town. Mostly they covered popular songs and old country standards, like those by Hank Williams, Johnny Cash, and Merle Haggard.

"You mentioned school. How does that fit in with everything else going on in your lives?" I ask.

"It's been a struggle at times," Chris says. "We went to a local elementary school and then Mom started to homeschool us when the band got more shows. We were fortunate that way. It allowed us to focus on the music and also make sure we could read and write," he says with a grin.

"I'm still finishing high school courses, actually," Lily says. "Chris finished last spring."

I ask if they have any college plans, but both say they aren't sure yet. They're really enjoying the music and want to see how they can grow and keep learning through their experiences with the band and writing music.

"Is it difficult to keep a calm, stable lifestyle as touring musicians?" I ask. "Many musicians say fame is hard to handle, especially when you're still in your teens."

"There are times when I wish I could get rid of the craziness, when the pace is just too fast," Lily explains. "But I'm also grateful for this experience and am trying to enjoy it as much as I can. Our parents are really good about helping us filter out the insanity of publicists, agents, lawyers, and all of that. And it helps to have a sibling in the band, I think. We're all pretty close. That helps."

"We try to be active in the community, too," Chris says. "We perform at local schools sometimes. And our parents are nature lovers. They instilled that in us. We help them with park clean-ups and some other things like that. It helps us to take our minds off of the business and to stay humble. Our dad is big on humility."

It's clear that their parents play an integral part in their lives. Throughout our conversation, each parent pops in to see how things are going, to refill beverages, and to relay phone messages. I ask Chris and Lily if they yearn to be independent, if they have plans to move to Nashville at some point.

"This works for us now," Chris says. "We actually like our parents and respect them. They helped us to be where we are today."

"Being on tour makes me appreciate coming back to the farm," Lily says. "I'm excited to turn eighteen, though, and I'd love to live in New York, or at least Nashville."

Chris nods in agreement while playing a few notes on his guitar. "It's really about the music for us. We love it and we want to keep at it—see where it goes," he says. "We don't want to disappear like a fad. We have faith that if we keep playing, trying to become the best musicians we can, we'll be happy. And we'll put on some darn good shows."

Lily had been tinkering with a few notes while Chris was talking. With only a nod from him, they launch into a song, a melodious instrumental that swoops and glides and soars, making this reporter ponder how the band name is so appropriate. It's a performance that definitely makes for a darn good show.

Campaign Poster

illustrated by Danielle Caruso

Even Better Butter

illustrated by Dion Williams

DOUBLE THE FUN IN HALF THE TIME!

peanut butter and grape jelly
peanut butter and strawberry jelly
peanut butter and banana
peanut butter and chocolate

Even Better Butter

Pocket Pals

illustrated by Dion Williams

Many scents to choose from!

Apple
Orange
Blueberry
Strawberry
Grape
Peanut Butter and Jelly
Banana Split
Orange Creamsicle
Marshmallow
Sugar Cookie Dough
Island Citrus
Coconut
Caribbean Sun
Ocean Breeze
Passion Flower

Pocket Pals

Hand sanitizers

Collect them all!

The Infinity

illustrated by Dion Williams

The possibilities are infinite.

Dutch Teen Completes Solo World Voyage

by Summer Swauger
illustrated by Megan Crow

January 22, 2012

PHILIPSBURG, St. Martin — Dutch teen Laura Dekker sailed into port in St. Martin last night, becoming the youngest person to sail alone around the world.

Dekker, 16, set sail from St. Martin on January 20, 2011, when she was 15 years old. She sailed her red 38-foot sailboat named *Guppy* for 27,000 nautical miles across three oceans. Just 366 days later, she completed her record-breaking voyage.

"It is overwhelming, too fantastic, and most of the time I don't believe it is really happening," Dekker wrote in her blog as her journey came to an end. "I am looking forward to my arrival and to officially ending my journey, even though I feel like I have already accomplished what I set out to do a long time ago."

Dekker's route began at the island of St. Martin in the Caribbean. She sailed through the Panama Canal and into the Pacific Ocean, where she visited several islands. She crossed the Pacific to Australia, passed through the Indian Ocean to South Africa, and sailed across the Atlantic Ocean back to St. Martin.

Even though she was alone, Dekker had much to do. She had to navigate her boat, withstand storms, and make repairs. At times, she had to chase away cockroaches. She also continued her studies while at sea through *Wereldschool* (Worldschool), which provides materials for self-taught learning.

The young sailor's trek wasn't all work, though. Dekker had time for cliff and scuba diving, surfing, and sightseeing. She also wrote a blog and learned to play the flute during her voyage. She even celebrated her birthday at sea.

"I have already learned very much about myself along the way, and I also have learned very much from all of the different places and the many different people I came in contact with in so many different countries," she wrote.

Sailing solo around the world at 15 may sound daunting; however, Dekker had been preparing for this challenge her entire life. She was born on her parents' boat, docked just off the coast of New Zealand. She spent the first four years of her life at sea with her parents, on a voyage around the globe.

Dekker received her first boat at age six and learned to sail soon after. By age 10, she was making solo voyages. Then, in 2009, at age 13, she sailed alone across the English Channel, from Maurik, Netherlands, to Lowestoft, England. In August of that same year, Dekker announced her plans for a two-year solo voyage around the world, a feat that would fulfill her lifelong dream.

Although Dekker's parents supported her decision, authorities in the Netherlands did not. Child welfare officials stepped in, saying that the trip was too dangerous for such a young person to attempt alone. A court ruling forced Dekker to postpone her trip until August 2010. After further court battles and objections from child welfare officials, Dekker won the right to begin her journey in September 2010, when she turned 15.

The long legal battle brought Dekker into the international spotlight. Media coverage, court hearings, and interviews with Dutch government officials left her distressed.

"It was never my intention to be the center of world news," she wrote on her blog. "From the moment my plans became public, Youth Care and other government organizations tried to stop me."

The Dutch government argued that it was only trying to protect Laura. "We had a duty to investigate," said Caroline Vink, of the Netherlands Youth Institute. "We never meant to make her life difficult, only to look out for her safety." Government officials insisted that Dekker's boat have the most up-to-date navigational technology and that she attend survival classes before she could be allowed to go.

Still, Dekker said that because of her experiences with the Dutch government, "I have the feeling that it will be very difficult for me to return to the Netherlands." As a result, she chose to end her world voyage in St. Martin instead of sailing back to the Netherlands.

Although Dekker claims to be the youngest person to complete a solo circumnavigation of the globe, the Guinness Book of World Records refused to officially recognize her voyage. The organization removed that category to discourage young people from trying such a dangerous venture. But Dekker never wanted fame.

"I did not start on my trip to achieve any record," she wrote in her blog. "I did it just for myself."

The last official record-holder in the youngest circumnavigator category is Michael Perham. In 2009, he set the record at age 17 in a 50-foot racing yacht.

Since then, others have unofficially broken Perham's record. Jessica Watson of Australia beat out Perham in May 2010, three days before she turned 17. American Abby Sunderland, then 16, also attempted the journey in 2010, but had to be rescued when her boat capsized in the Indian Ocean. Dekker was six months younger than Watson when she sailed into port, beating Watson's record and making history.

Since completing her trip, Dekker is easing back into her life. She said that she would like to live in New Zealand rather than return to the Netherlands. She plans to finish her schooling. She is also writing a book about her adventure.

Dekker is considering working in conservation, a cause that she believes in. During her trip, she raised money for Sea Shepherd, an international organization that protects ocean wildlife. But most importantly, she plans to continue sailing.

"I had no idea I would be back now with a life load of new experiences," she wrote, reflecting on her journey. For Dekker, it is still hard to believe. "I sailed around the world and I am still surprised that it just feels so incredibly normal."

To read Dekker's first-hand accounts of her journey, visit her blog at http://www.lauradekker.nl/English/Home.html.

SEVEN WONDERS OF THE ANCIENT WORLD

The Seven Wonders of the Ancient World

by Summer Swauger
illustrated by Dion Williams

February 2012

Ancient writers and philosophers wrote about the great accomplishments of their civilizations. They kept lists of the most amazing creations of their time. One of those lists survives today. It is called the Seven Wonders of the Ancient World. While many people have heard of this list, few can name any of the structures on it. Only one of these ancient wonders still exists today, but all seven have earned their places in history. They remain some of mankind's greatest works.

The Great Pyramid of Giza, Egypt

The Great Pyramid stands in Giza, Egypt. It is the oldest of the seven ancient wonders. It is also the only one that still exists. Built around 2560 B.C., it is thought to have been designed as a tomb for the Pharaoh Khufu. Egyptians believed that the Pharaohs were living gods. They buried their rulers in elaborate tombs filled with treasures. Scientists have tried to guess how such a huge architectural task was completed without modern technology. No one knows for sure, however. Khufu's

Pyramid measures 450 feet high. It is made of more than two million blocks of limestone, each weighing approximately 2.5 tons. Inside are hidden rooms and secret passageways. Pharaoh Khufu's body and treasure have not been found within the pyramid.

The Hanging Gardens of Babylon, Iraq

The mythical Hanging Gardens are said to have once stood in the ancient city of Babylon, in what is now Iraq. Thought to have been built around 600 B.C., the gardens were a gift from Nebuchadnezzar, king of Babylon, to his wife. The gardens are said to have been terraced, with one level on top of another. Since Babylon received very little rain, the gardens were likely irrigated with water from the nearby Euphrates River. Water was hauled to the top terrace and then released so that it ran down onto each terrace below. Remains of the Hanging Gardens have never been found. They are the only ancient wonder whose existence cannot be proven.

The Statue of Zeus at Olympia, Greece

Zeus was the mythological king of the Greek gods who lived on Mount Olympus. Every four years, the Greeks held a festival of athletics to honor Zeus. This festival was called the Olympic Games, a tradition that is still kept today. Near the site of this festival was a temple dedicated to Zeus. Around 432 B.C., the sculptor Phidias was chosen to create a statue to go inside the temple. Twelve years later, the completed statue stood more than forty feet tall. That was almost as high as the temple itself. Made of ivory and gold, it showed Zeus seated on his throne. Some believe that the statue was damaged by earthquakes and fires. A few of the temple's columns still remain, but nothing is left of the mighty statue.

The Colossus of Rhodes, Greece

Built over two thousand years ago, the Colossus was a 110-foot bronze statue. It was dedicated to Helios, Greek god of the sun. It stood at the harbor entrance on the Greek island of Rhodes. It was built around 290 B.C. to celebrate Rhodes's victory over invading armies. Some suggest that the statue stood on a pedestal, wore a spiked crown, and held a torch in its right hand. Today, the Statue of Liberty in New York harbor is sometimes referred to as the "Modern Colossus" because it stands in the same pose. The Colossus collapsed when an earthquake hit Rhodes in 226 B.C. The people of Rhodes thought Helios was offended and destroyed the statue. They never rebuilt it. Huge pieces of the great Colossus were scattered on the ground for centuries. Eventually, the pieces were taken by invaders and sold.

The Lighthouse of Alexandria, Egypt

This great lighthouse was called the Pharos for the small island it stood on. Constructed around 290 B.C., it was the first lighthouse ever built. It was located in Alexandria, Egypt. Standing at more than 450 feet high, it guided countless ships into harbor. The Pharos had three levels, all made of stone. At the top was an open part where fire burned day and night. The fire light was reflected off of a bronze mirror. The mirror sent a beacon of light out to sea. It was said that the light could be seen up to one hundred miles away. The Pharos remained a tourist attraction in Egypt for centuries. Sadly, it was destroyed by an earthquake in 1375 A.D.

The Mausoleum of Mausolus at Halicarnassus, Turkey

The great mausoleum was erected around 350 B.C. It was a tomb for Mausolus, governor of the city of Halicarnassus. The tomb was commissioned by his wife, Artemisia. The building was of Greek design and it sat on a hill overlooking Halicarnassus. It was made of marble and decorated with columns, statues, and sculptures. The roof held statues of Mausolus and Artemisia riding in a chariot pulled by four horses. The building was so famous that the word *mausoleum*, which comes from the name Mausolus, now refers to any grand tomb. The mausoleum stood in Halicarnassus until 1404 A.D., when an earthquake destroyed it. A few of the statues survived, however. They are now housed in the British Museum in London, England.

The Temple of Artemis at Ephesus, Turkey

The Temple of Artemis, in what was then the Greek city of Ephesus, was dedicated to the goddess Artemis. The temple was destroyed and rebuilt several times on the site, but the great temple that was erected there in 323 B.C. was by far the largest. It had 127 columns. Inside the temple were many statues, carvings, and other works of art. Philo of Byzantium, a Greek writer, said of the temple, "I have seen the walls and Hanging Gardens of ancient Babylon, the statue of Olympian Zeus, the Colossus of Rhodes, the mighty work of the high Pyramids and the tomb of Mausolus. But when I saw the temple at Ephesus rising to the clouds, all these other wonders were put in the shade." But in 268 A.D., the mighty temple was destroyed by invaders. Some pieces of the temple can be seen in the British Museum. All that remains at the temple site, though, are a few chunks of crumbled marble.

About the Authors

Patricia Bernard is a curriculum specialist at the National Network of Digital Schools (NNDS). She has worked as a teacher and tutor for grades 1 – 12 in Massachusetts, and educated her son at home until he began cyber schooling. Ms. Bernard is a beekeeper, gardener, and reader, and she enjoys constructing collage poetry. She lives in Pittsburgh, PA, with her husband, son, dog, cat, and the wildlife in their forested yard.

Nicole Costlow works as the Editing Coordinator for the Middle and Secondary Curriculum Department at NNDS. She resides in Hopewell Township, PA, with her husband, Chuck, and her cat, Shiloh. When Nicole is not writing or editing, she enjoys traveling, skiing, hiking, camping, and spending time with her family.

Jill Fisher has always had a passion for school and a desire to help others. Before writing educational curriculum, she worked as an elementary school teacher. Mrs. Fisher loves to spend time with her family and friends. She is also active in her community and her daughters' school. She currently lives in her small hometown of Toronto, OH, with her husband, Billy, and her precious daughters, Riley, Chloe, and Sydney.

Sarah Marino is an editor and a writer at NNDS. She has worked as an editor at Google in California and as a website content manager at Shadyside Academy in Pittsburgh, PA. She has been writing poems and stories since childhood. When she's not reading or writing, she enjoys running on the trails of Pittsburgh's parks, trying interesting foods, and spending time with family and friends.

Debbie Parrish is retired from a thirty-five-year career as an elementary school educator. She always enjoyed writing original stories and poems to use in her classroom to encourage the "inner author" in her students. Mrs. Parrish is the mother of four grown children, and she loves being "Grandma" to her four lively grandchildren. When not busy at home in Elkin, NC, she and her husband enjoy traveling and having new adventures, both inside and outside of the United States.

Michael Scotto wrote his first story when he was four years old. Today, he is the author of the Tales of Midlandia picture book series, *Postcards from Pismo*, and the *Latasha* novel series. In his spare time, he enjoys speaking with students, cooking, and photography. A graduate of Carnegie Mellon University, he currently lives in Pittsburgh, PA, with his wife and their very naughty dog.

Summer Swauger is very excited to be working as an elementary content editor for NNDS. In the past, she has written for newspapers, newsletters, websites, and marketing projects. She has performed in several musicals and even appeared in a major motion picture. She enjoys reading, knitting, crocheting, and gardening. Summer lives in Pittsburgh, PA, with her husband, Jason, and their adorable dog, Daisy.